MESSY FAITH

DARING TO LIVE BY GRACE

A. J. GREGORY

Revell

a division of Baker Publishing Group
Grand Rapids, Michigan

Published by Revell
a division of Baker Publishing Group
P.O. Box 6287, Grand Rapids, MI 49516–6287
www.revellbooks.com

Printed in the United States of America

Library of Congress Cataloging-in-Publication Data
Gregory, A. J., 1976–
   Messy faith : daring to live by grace / A.J. Gregory.
      p. cm.
   Includes bibliographical references.
   ISBN 978-0-8007-3284-4 (pbk.)
      1. Grace (Theology) 2. Christian life. I. Title.
   BT761.3.G74 2008
   234'.1—dc22   2008026153

CONTENTS

To all those who want to believe.

ACKNOWLEDGMENTS

Thank you to . . .

My family. Mom, you are a true survivor and have taught me how to be a strong woman. Jimmy, your talent has been the soundtrack behind many of these pages. Vivien, thank you for always believing in me and being my best friend (and having an adventurous spirit). Jordan, your faith that the sky is the limit is refreshing and always makes me smile. Uncle Steve, your faith is an inspiration.

My literary agent, Esther Fedorkevich. You are the best agent in the world. I am in awe of your persistence and your passion.

The dedicated, talented, and hardworking staff at Baker Publishing Group who helped *Messy Faith* happen. Jennifer Leep, thank you for believing in my writing and being the advocate for this book.

Doyline. For being there through all my messes. Never stop believing.

INTRODUCTION

I got a tattoo on my wrist today. I've wanted it for a while. It says "trust" in beautiful script. My tattoo artist and I had it out because he was convinced the tattoo was for other people and so it should face opposite of me. I was floored. I wanted it to face me. I wanted to look at it because I needed to be reminded of it . . . all the time. It's the most incredible tattoo of all the ones I have.

Trust.

I've needed to learn to trust in God throughout my faith journey. It has been a difficult thing to do for many reasons, and, at times as a result, my sojourn has been messy. Messy but beautiful. Make no doubt, the two are intertwined, and it took me a long time to really believe it.

I was watching the VH1 show *Celebrity Rehab* the other day, the reality TV show that filmed the recovery process of famous addicts. One of the big names on the show was Seth "Shifty" Binzer, the lead singer from the band Crazytown, who was addicted to cocaine and crack for years. A video clip showed him smoking crack on his way into rehab. On one particular episode, toward the tail end of the show, the group was out at a coffeehouse open mic night. Shifty performed a rap, and one of the lines he spouted out really struck me. "I'm dancing in the ashes of the riches I've burned." I thought it was the most profound thing I'd heard in a long time, and it reminded me of my life. Through my messes, past and even current, I feel like I'm dancing in the garbage that God has transformed into beauty.

I've had a strong faith in God for most of my life. My trust has been in God because there is no way I could trust myself. I'm not saying I did the right things all of the time or that my faith was necessarily solid most times. My faith—sometimes looking like a speck of dust, other times looking as solid as the Lincoln memorial—has been there. Blurry and clear, weak and strong, full of passionate fire, a smoking ember . . . it has been present. I've always believed in God because I couldn't not believe in Him.

This book isn't about me. I've tried very hard not to make it seem like my story matters so much. Honestly, who cares about my struggles? Who cares about the journey of faith I stumbled through like a sloppy drunk? Who cares about the monkeys that lurked on my back? And who really cares about my revelation? These are the questions I have asked myself as I wrote about what I call messy faith.

But this book isn't about me, really, it's about all of your stories. It's about your journey with God. And it's about trying to reconcile your pains, your doubts, your questions, your imperfections, your vices, and your lapses with faith in an invisible God. While I don't diminish my personal and unique circumstances, my hope is that whatever I share is at least transparent enough so your story is visible.

Messy Faith addresses the muddled adventure that working out our faith in God can sometimes look like. It is being sure and unsure, whole and broken, warring, losing and winning. It is being right and being wrong and having no clue, but believing anyway. And it is trusting in God for perfecting the final product—our flawed, human selves.

We are all searching for the right way to live out Christianity. And while we have the Bible as a handbook, there are some issues, questions, and challenges that it does not directly or thoroughly discuss. While the appeals to "just believe" and "go and sin no more" and "love your enemies" seem obvious enough, why does it feel so difficult, if not impossible, to practically engage them into our lives?

How does the alcoholic, for instance, instantaneously snap away the addiction with his trembling fingers? How does he arbitrate his love for God when it is constantly playing fatal war games with his need for a drink? How does a young lady deal with a temptation that she has furiously prayed about but just won't go away? How does she reconcile her want to serve God with the beckoning breath of the forbidden? How does a long-time Christian, who believes the message of the gospel to be convicting not condemning, still suffer from the shackles of legalism? How does he fall into and rest in Love's open arms when his flesh shrieks of unworthiness? These are the folks to whom *Messy Faith* speaks.

Messiness does not only appear in individual circumstances that spark combat between our spirits and flesh, but in life's daily bustle and doldrums—in our communion with others, in our office complexes, in our homes, and in our prayer closets. What does faith look like when people bore us to death or are simply annoying? When work stresses have pillaged our sense of wonder and joy? When dealing with our five-year-old twins has turned our hair prematurely gray? When prayer seems more like a burden than a sanctum?

Within these life-areas is where the challenge of being a Christian falls—being carriers of the presence of God and accommodating Him in broken, clay pots of flesh and blood, tissue and muscle. And while God, through his spirit, enables us to live according to his good purposes, we must not forget the shells of our humanity. They exist; they do not vanish when we become believers. And they usually interfere with our false illusions of the perfect Christian.

Let's be honest. Ours can be a messy faith. While most of us trudge toward the Cross with the best of intentions, our lives, at times, are not played out that way. We all fall short in some area and, therefore, need to rely on Christ to perfect us in his image. This is what *Messy Faith* explores—the bedraggled and unkempt shadows of the journey of belief. While in our eyes our faith may look bandaged, scraped, bruised, and busted, in God's eyes, and because of him, our faith is made whole.

It is my prayer that you find your resting place of trust in a God you cannot see. That you keep believing in him when everything around you tells you not to. That you keep hoping he will work in your life so that even that trash you may have sown becomes a treasure beyond your deepest imagination. I don't care how messy your life is right now, know that if you keep your faith, whatever it may look like, you will dance even in the ashes of the riches you may have burned.

1

WANTED:
SPIRITUAL MASOCHISTS

In life as in dance: Grace glides on blistered feet.

Alice Abrams

I used to be a spiritual masochist. I would have rather gotten whipped by God than freely received the foreign gifts of mercy and grace. Every time I messed up or did something stupid, I wished to hear a booming voice from heaven—appropriately accompanied by a trembling iron fist, a soundtrack of roaring thunder, and sharp flashes of blinding lightning—bark at my frailties and literally scare the living daylights out of me. I hoped for some visible evidence of punishment: a slap on the wrist, a kick in the butt, maybe even a broken leg from a car accident. I imagined it was necessary to make reparations for my messy journey of faith.

For many years I took refuge under an umbrella of fear. My spirituality wasn't healthy. I was mainly afraid, among other things, that my life would be ruined by one wrong move. Or a bad decision. Or a genuine misinterpretation of Scripture. Or an unplanned detour. Or an addiction I wasn't successful at curing overnight.

And suddenly, I was sure, God's exasperated groan would violently jar the serenity of heaven, and Saint Peter would start scratching my name off of the list of people who were called to fulfill some sort of marvelous destiny. The former disciple who suffered from chronic foot-in-mouth disease would shake his head and start rattling off an I-told-you-so speech: "I told you, God. Listen, A. J. was always a little wild. She's too hard to control. You know that passion in life, that *je ne sais quoi* she was created with? Well, she was always more likely to use it for worldly pleasures than your glory. Stick with the gals who don't like to laugh a lot and have a good time."

But really, were my shortcomings such a radical surprise to God? If he knows such intricate yet practically useless information as the exact number of hairs on my head (see Matt. 10:30), was he too blind to notice the weaknesses that anxiously squirmed in the dark corners of my being? Did my imperfections really make him gasp in astonishment? Was he really that floored when I messed up?

During the years I spent envisioning a cantankerous and hostile God, my faith walk was sadly eclipsed by dread and unease. After all, I believed I served a God who lacked kindness and understanding. A God who demanded I try to reach clearly unattainable expectations and who became a demanding disciplinarian when I failed miserably. A God whose compassion and, more importantly, grace had a definite beginning and end—and I imagined the distance between the two to be embarrassingly short, at least for me.

While I understood that coming to Christ was only made possible through grace, I needed to be reminded that grace would be a perpetual force throughout the entire journey. Grace didn't just show up to work as a temp. No, she was there for the long haul. While to some degree I knew this in theory, the concept didn't successfully connect with my heart.

We are saved by grace not because of ourselves, Paul reminded us, but because of God. Grace is what has allowed us to crawl or nosedive our way into becoming a follower of Christ. But I believe, as I have seen it evidenced in the lives of so many people, that we tragically forget that saying the ABC prayer of salvation does not suddenly make us any less human than we were before. Many of us still wrestle with the same kinds of addictions, temptations, thoughts, and feelings. It is just that now we have the spiritual freedom to live without needing to exert all our energies trying to reach perfection, a holy utopia. We have the unconditional support of a God who "longs to be gracious to [us]; he rises to show [us] compassion" (Isa. 30:18). We suddenly have an advocate who is rooting for us and who even intercedes on our behalf (see John 17:20–26).

That being said, we can't ignore Paul's mandate not to use our "freedom to satisfy [our] sinful nature" (Gal. 5:13 NLT). Living with grace—as I'm sure you have heard many times before—is not a license to do as the Romans do. Most of us know a man or woman who purposefully does the same stupid things over and over again. They run to the altar every Sunday drenched in faux tears and the perverse reassurance of a guilty conscience, only to hightail it back to their destructive breeding grounds just days later. Subconsciously aware that grace will be waiting for them next week, they rush to immediately satisfy the hankering ache in their bellies. So they do what they do best. They ignore the loving voice of caution and return to their own vomit (see Prov. 26:11).

Anyone committed to the Christian faith knows not to take grace for granted, and yet many Christians are so afraid of abusing grace that they defensively develop an immunity to it. And for some the concept of love and grace has been so grossly polluted by their own life experience that the truth that "God is love" is equally as marred. And some simply feel they don't deserve grace.

In your spiritual journey, have you slipped up? Stumbled? Still don't quite "get it"? Do you struggle with spiritual disciplines? Are you painfully progressing toward recovery at a snail's pace? Do you beat yourself up for these things? Do you feel so unworthy and disappointed in yourself that you would rather see God kicking or yelling at you than hugging and loving you?

It's such an awful place to be, isn't it? I like what the English writer William Hazlitt once wrote: "Grace is the absence of everything that indicates pain or difficulty, hesitation or incongruity."[1] And certainly that's the kind of grace we are afforded as followers of Jesus. So why is it so much easier to relate to pain and suffering than love and mercy? What is it about grace that makes us so uncomfortable?

We choose to live in fear rather than in freedom for many reasons. I know my own story involves many, and I'm sure yours does too. Rather than get into the obvious—like the difficulty in relating to our heavenly Father because of the sexually abusive earthly father we had; or growing up without a healthy concept of unconditional love; or having the awful experience of serving in a legalistic, fire-and-brimstone church—let me share what I learned was a big part of my problem.

While I knew I had to stop picturing God as a senseless dictator who paid more attention to my failures than my attempts,

I was wrestling with something even deeper. For ten years I suffered from an eating disorder and, as a textbook case for the disease, I overindulged in other destructive habits and behaviors to speed up the anesthetizing effects. After my gut-wrenching process of recovery, I had these random urges to return to my own harmful breeding grounds. These feelings were understandable, of course, but I couldn't handle them. I felt like a failure. A terrible Christian. An unholy mess. I was obviously doing something wrong.

My recovery itself wasn't a cakewalk. I had my fair share of slipups. When those moments came, I hid from God. I was thoroughly disgusted with every pore of my being. The shame was so unbearable that for days afterward I could barely look at my repulsive self in the mirror. When I did, all I saw were the words: FAILURE. SCREW-UP. UNWORTHY. A MISTAKE. PATHETIC. A POOR EXCUSE FOR A WOMAN. I was tormented by the thought, *If people knew who you truly were and saw you as the stinking piece of garbage you really are . . .*

Of course I always immediately prayed for forgiveness and repeated an eighteen-mile string of "I'm-sorrys." But what good would grace do? God telling me he forgave me meant nothing. Besides, it was my fault, and I was the one who had to live with the guilt and memory of messing up. I had to own my failures and roll in the mire for as long as it took for the shame to naturally dissipate. Needless to say, it was a wearisome time.

One day after one of my particularly intense sessions of self-loathing hate and weeping in repentance, something stirred in the depths of my spirit. Interesting questions surfaced. While you will never find me boasting "God told me _____" on a megaphone, I do believe he speaks to us. Most times it's in a still, small voice, and at least for me, it's usually brief but definitely poignant.

There I was, mutilating my self-esteem with poisonous words and cussing like a sailor at God for creating such a monster, when I heard, "Why are you slipping up? What's going on? And why on earth do you hate yourself so much? Why, A. J., why?" I froze. I wasn't expecting questions. I was expecting the bad feelings to just go away. See, that's what I thought the point of forgiveness was. In coming to God with a sincerely repentant heart, I had foolishly hoped that after I was absolved of my wrong, the discomfort of guilt and shame would do a disappearing act. But that wasn't the case. Accepting divine atonement meant really thinking about what I had done. Not in a perverse, judgmental way but by being guided by the gentle hands of the Holy Spirit in meditation on my destructive behavior and addictive habits.

That's why I so desperately craved actual punishment or physical judgment after asking for forgiveness. Paying for Sin A with Atonement B was something I could see, do, and manage. I didn't have to delve into my being to reflect on my messed-up motives and the underlying needs I was trying to superficially meet. I now believe that true repentance doesn't come without taking some measure of responsibility. True repentance means hunkering down to figure out why we are doing what we are doing and what it is going to take to discontinue the same sickly pattern.

Remember the story of the woman caught in the act of adultery that is told in the Gospel of John? Here we have a woman getting it on with a married man when, all of a sudden, she is violently seized out of the bed by a group of holier-than-thou Pharisees. With satisfied smirks on their faces, they drag the kicking and screaming woman away and go find Jesus. While what she did was clearly wrong, the religious elect weren't making an example out of her to uphold the sanctity of marriage. They just wanted to use her immorality to trick Jesus into a debate about sin, law, and capital punishment.

As they continue to publicly humiliate this disheveled woman, they approach Jesus with a distorted respect for the law and feign innocent expressions. "Hey there, Jesus. Look who we found fornicating with a man who isn't her own. What shall we do with this floozy, Teacher? Stone her? Isn't that what the law says?" Some of them start massaging the sharp edges of the rocks that line their pockets.

Jesus wisely keeps his mouth shut and starts to write something in the dirt with his fingers. His silence is deafening to the Pharisees, so they keep pestering him about whether or not to initiate the stone-throwing fest. Finally their eyes catch sight of what Jesus has written on the ground. While we don't know for sure what it said, it was powerful enough to prompt a resonating echo as rocks tumbled out of their grimy hands and hit the ground with thunderous thuds. One by one these self-righteous bigots—masking faces flushed with anger and frustration—turn on their heels and bolt in the opposite direction of Jesus and the scarlet woman. "Then Jesus stood up again and said to the woman, 'Where are your accusers? Didn't even one of them condemn you?' 'No, Lord,' she said. And Jesus said, 'Neither do I. Go and sin no more'" (John 8:10–11 NLT).

It's quite a lofty command, isn't it—that "go and sin no more" bit? Let's think about this for a moment. There are some things that we should not do because they are just stupid, have weighty consequences, will ruin innocent lives in the process, and, more importantly, violate God's moral codes. Some of those things, though challenging, are quite manageable to give up, say no to, or even avoid.

But some other things are pretty impossible to simply stop doing all of a sudden unless we seek some sort of professional intervention or spiritual guidance. If you are an alcoholic who wants to begin recovery, it almost seems absurd to just stop drinking out of the clear blue. If you are a womanizer, chances are you won't wake up one morning with a Dear John letter from your sexual urges. (If you are one of those lucky people who got saved and were instantly delivered from your bad habits, nasty thoughts, and addictive behaviors, praise God. But you are few and far between and not the type of person I am addressing here.)

I think that what a part of "I forgive you, now go and sin no more" really means is confronting the behaviors or feelings that may have contributed to the acting out of sin. I hear Jesus saying something like this to us: "You are forgiven. My love for you is the same. We're cool. Now, why did you do what you did? What's really going on in your messy, troubled, anxiety-ridden heart that we need to talk about? What kind of internal work do you have to do to stop living the kind of life that is ultimately bringing you ruin, destruction, and general unhealth?"

Being punished by a physical or tangible consequence seemed easier than having to internalize my actions and behavior. But knowing I had to work at spiritual self-development? That I had to actually do some homework and figure out, like what Paul wrestled with in Romans 7, why I do what I don't want to do and don't do what I should do? Good grief! I wanted to be sent wailing to a whipping post instead.

Let me make a suggestion to you: instead of thumbing through the eighty or so books that line your bookshelves about how to be a better Christian, how to avoid temptation, how to stop judging, how to be less selfish, and how to get out of negative thought patterns, sit in the dark and meditate about why you believe you do those things. Instead of following a four-step, cookie-cutter plan to become a better person, allow Jesus to challenge the internal issues that you'd rather not bring to light because of the sheer terror of seeing them naked and exposed. Instead of repeating a cutesy phrase you learned in Sunday school (like "When the devil knocks at your door, tell Jesus to open it"), rest at the feet of the greatest psychologist in the universe. Because when the devil knocks at your door and you expect Jesus to open it and shoo him away, you are experiencing a naive and superficial faith that just may detonate at any time into a million tiny pieces. Besides, no offense, but Jesus is not your doorman.

And hey, I'm not suggesting that you *not* read the Bible or an inspirational self-help book or that you avoid therapists like the plague. I'm just saying that sometimes we have deeper issues that only God can surgically heal through time, through asking a lot of questions, and through our willingness to work out the hard stuff. Our source of hope is that Jesus doesn't approach our screw-ups with condemnation. He does call us to start thinking about what we need to do to avoid repeating our careless routines. And he requires us to be honest. Admit that you are lonely. Stare head-on at whatever fear is haunting you. Confess your frailties. It's the only way to truly and fully accept forgiveness and grace.

What Do We Really Deserve Anyway?

My rumble with spiritual masochism didn't just involve the difficulty of receiving forgiveness and grace or learning it was actually better to "work out" your spirituality instead of relying on punishment to find peace. The destructive and legalistic impulses also crept up when good things happened to me. Or when my prayers got answered. Or when it seemed God's faithfulness was being harvested in my life. All that goodness and joy felt somewhat weird, out of place, and definitely undeserved.

So I got nervous and assumed that somehow God got the wrong message. I was sure that instead of being the recipient of a good gift from my heavenly Father, I should have gotten a sack of coal, or at least the familiar wind from the slam of another closed door. I started to think that whatever assistant God hired to keep him up-to-date with what's going on in my life must have gotten their paperwork mixed up. I was erroneously ascribed to the good list instead of the bad list.

The problem was not that I was engaging in a lifestyle contrary to what Jesus calls us to and thus felt convicted of doing something wrong. I wasn't guilty of tax evasion. I wasn't smoking crack. I wasn't prostituting myself on my church corner. I was simply confused.

Weren't you supposed to merit good stuff? If I went to church every Sunday, was faithfully involved in some ministry, prayed every day on my knees for three hours, didn't wear too much makeup, and got more excited about door-to-door evangelizing than a day at the spa, then I could understand and even justify God-given life pleasantries. But I was just a regular Christian doing the best I could to have a more intimate relationship with Christ. And I was dragging my haunting past into that space. For many different reasons, I was used to feeling like everything I did was wrong or not good enough. I had lived my life for so long with proven formulas and equations that made sense. So good stuff happening as a result of a not-so-perfect life seemed plain wrong.

What did I do? What any paranoid, overanalytical, and broken woman would do. I put together a list of all the reasons why God shouldn't bless me, and I recited it to him with great passion. I reminded him about the mistakes I have made and do make. Drumroll, please. . . . Remember when I drank so much I threw up in that country club? Remember when I abused my insides and

24

squandered my emotional and mental health by being bulimic for ten years? Remember when I tried cocaine? Remember how long it took for me to develop a stable devotional life? Remember when I was a closet smoker? Remember how last week I couldn't stop staring at one of my clients' muscular arms? Remember when I fantasized about Viggo Mortensen taking me out to dinner?

On many occasions, I rambled on and on incessantly, comparing my religious and life track record to what I thought I deserved, and I never found any equilibrium. I talked about a wide range of stuff. From bad choices I made years ago to what I believed was my own superficiality because of my appreciation of fashion and nice things. I'll be honest: I got sick and tired of the self-diatribe. It didn't make me feel better. It didn't strengthen my spirituality. It didn't make me think of how I could better myself. But it did stir up a desire to slit my wrists out of sheer frustration.

But I started thinking one day: if it's true that "there is none righteous, no, not one" (Rom. 3:10 KJV), if "not a single person on earth is always good and never sins" (Eccles. 7:20 NLT), if we all so desperately have the need "to be found in Him, not having [our] own righteousness, which is from the law, but that which is through faith in Christ, the righteousness which is from God by faith" (Phil. 3:9 NKJV), then even if I was perfect, it wouldn't matter anyway. According to the Bible, apart from Christ, our righteousness has the clout of a filthy rag. There is no debit and credit system to what we feel we do or do not deserve.

I am very aware that good or bad consequences do naturally result from doing good or bad things. If you speed on a highway, you may have to pay a hefty fine. If you swap sexual partners every three days, you have a greater chance of getting an STD. If you kill someone, you'll probably go to jail for the rest of your life. I am also very aware that life doesn't always work out how we think it should. Life isn't fair. Kids are dying from starvation all over the world. I know a woman whose husband got killed in a plane crash two weeks after they got married. A friend of mine is on her third consecutive miscarriage.

I finally gave up trying to explain away the good or bad that happens with an algebraic formula. It doesn't work. The writer of Ecclesiastes concludes, "The race is not to the swift or the battle to the strong, nor does food come to the wise or wealth to the brilliant or favor to the learned; but time and chance happen to them all" (9:11).

I am not implying that since none of us knows what tomorrow will bring, we should drown ourselves in our wicked indulgences. I'm offering that living our life in Christ means that in good times, bad times, fun times, unfair times, giddy times, depressing times, peaceful times, and empty times we are to do the best we can, give thanks in all things, and accept his love, mercy, and grace—whether or not we feel like we deserve it.

So getting back to the issue of what we do or do not deserve: have you ever truly thought about it? It's a tough question to honestly meditate on, let alone answer. Do I "deserve" to fall in love? Do I "deserve" to be in good health? Do I "deserve" not to reap a consequence of what I sow when my neighbor, who did the same thing as me, is now dealing with some agonizing repercussions? Do I "deserve" something better or worse than the young lady sitting two pews down from me in church? Do I "deserve" an instantaneous miracle? Do I "deserve" to have all my prayers answered?

For that matter, do you?

I think what I deserve is to trust God in all things. To give him custody of my circumstances, my dreams, my desires, and my life. I deserve to be honest and authentic in my walk with him and to allow him to repair my brokenness and to make straight my crookedness. I deserve to rest in peace instead of wrestle with unanswerable questions. I deserve to be surprised at his leadings instead of forcing him to act out my poorly-written script. Perhaps one of the hardest things to accept is that I deserve to let go of my mistakes, to mourn my losses and finally put my shambles to rest. I deserve to bury the sins I have been forgiven for. Why? Simply because he says so. If we are truly repentant of what we have done wrong, what happens? Does God keep a list of those things in his file cabinet for future purposes? Does he go through a database of old sins, compare them with the new ones, and get frustrated that we still haven't learned our lesson in entirety? Does he whip out a flip chart and start tabulating the number of times we have asked for forgiveness?

Hebrews 8:12 tells us that he "will forgive their wickedness and will remember their sins no more." The book of Jeremiah agrees: "For I will forgive their iniquity, and their sin I will remember no more" (31:34 NKJV). Isaiah writes that the Lord says, "I, even I, am He who blots out your transgressions for My own sake; and I will not remember your sins" (Isa. 43:25 NKJV). If God forgets them, why don't we? Why do we torture ourselves by constantly replaying slow-motion clips of when and how we messed up?

Maybe the word "deserve" is not the best word to use for all of these things, but I believe these are the gifts that he gives us. These are the gifts that have more eternal weight and worth than that new house, that fancy car, that hot spouse, or that corner office with a view. He gives us an invitation, whether or not we feel we merit holding it in our shaky hands.

What a waste of emotions and energies when we beat ourselves into a bloody pulp and refuse to fall into Love's open arms. I'm not a theologian, by any means, but I am sure that doing that has got to be some sort of sin. Spiritual masochism certainly doesn't offer us any benefits except the guarantee of self-sabotage and misery.

The Voice in the Wilderness

In trying to gain a healthy understanding of God and his love, I have found myself drawn to the book of Isaiah, which at first glance may seem like quite an unlikely source of consolation. The writer of this Old Testament book is considered a poetic prophet and spoke about various God-given visions of destruction and blessing that related to the broken nation of Israel. Isaiah's message—in addition to the telling of some messianic prophecies—was one of repentance and of a hope that God would deliver his people. John Oswalt writes in his commentary that the book of Isaiah "contains an unparalleled sweep of theology, all the way from creation to the new heavens and new earth and from utter destruction to glorious redemption."[2] Isaiah is a beautiful piece of writing.

Perhaps I found my refuge in these Scriptures because I could relate to the Israelites. I know I've sure messed up as many times as those folks. I've been in plenty of sticky situations as a result of my own stupid decisions. I have misused what I was supposed to wisely steward. I have wandered aimlessly in the desert for longer than necessary because I was too scared to give God my compass and let him guide me through the sandstorms. My idolatry of addiction served as a barricade to prevent me from experiencing God fully. The frustration that was birthed from waiting on what seemed like an absent God kept me running in the opposite direction, trying to get things done faster on my own.

The specific themes of hope and deliverance expectantly color the lyrical prose of the passages I meditated on, particularly this one:

> "Comfort, oh comfort my people,"
>   says your God.
> "Speak softly and tenderly to Jerusalem,
>   but also make it very clear
> That she has served her sentence,
>   that her sin is taken care of—forgiven!
> She's been punished enough and more than enough,
>   and now it's over and done with."
> Thunder in the desert!
>   "Prepare for God's arrival!
> Make the road straight and smooth,
>   a highway fit for our God.
> Fill in the valleys,
>   level off the hills,
> Smooth out the ruts,
>   clear out the rocks.
> Then God's bright glory will shine
>   and everyone will see it.
>   Yes. Just as God has said."
>
> Isaiah 40:1–5 Message

The message that was being dispatched to the Israelites, who were disconnected from God for a number of reasons, was God had not left them and was planning on showing up in a big way. They would even be his witnesses to trumpet the sovereignty of the Lord to the kingdoms that clutched the invisible hands of false gods and buried their hearts deep into the soil of idolatry. God was going to bring them back home where they belonged.

Other translations tell of a voice that cried out, "Listen! It's the voice of someone shouting, 'Clear the way through the wilderness for the LORD! Make a straight highway through the wasteland for our God!'" (Isa. 40:3 NLT). It is through our own individual wildernesses and wastelands that we find the exodus toward freedom, restoration, and the abundance of life. How do we prepare the way for the Lord to reveal his truth, his love, and his redemption when the voices of our masochism and worthlessness viciously compete with his welcoming arrival? How do we manage to silence the ear-splitting curses saying that we only deserve a kick in the pants?

Believe. Believe in the God who is love. Or at least believe in that God more than the one you have created out of your abyss of despair. Give your crumbling faith a push so the voice of hope speaks louder than your inner demons and outer critics.

I was sitting in my car one day, inspecting each piece of debris that I had sown in my life and entertaining every possible negative thought and emotion that surfaced. In the midst of my mental beating, a voice in my spirit lamented with such anguish it was impossible to ignore: "Do you think that's me? Do you really believe I am reminding you of all of that junk? Do you really think that's the kind of God I am? Do you really believe I believe those negative things about you? Do you really feel I don't think anything will ever work out for you? Do you really believe I don't love you? Do you really believe I don't care? Do you really believe that I am not even here?"

And in the hollow of my wrongs, my foolishness, my selfishness, my lapses in judgment, my fears, my anxieties, and my pain, I answered him back by calling myself every bad name in the book. "Well, God, you created this bleepity-bleep-bleep. How can you even look at such a bleepity-bleep-bleeping-bleep?"

Then I heard something else. It was quiet. Gentle. "This is not who *I* say you are."

You tend to fall apart in moments like that, when the Holy Spirit gently slices through your twisted defenses so that truth can seep through the tears and shed light in the dark. And surely it was true. Surely I was not the pathetic loser whose self-portrait I painted.

In that moment, I knew I couldn't bear to carry the burden of spiritual masochism any longer. I knew I had to make a life-changing decision. If I was to truly believe in God, if I was to devote my life to believing in his goodness and reflecting that same kind of mercy to others, then I had to pay closer attention to what he was whispering in my spirit.

Well, I wept like a baby, and with whatever small, human capacity of understanding I had at that moment, I got it. Most of us are much too hard on ourselves. God didn't call us to crucify ourselves with guilt, to martyr our joy with the sins of our youth, or to spend the rest of eternity paying for the damage we've done. Listen, there is an appropriate time for judgment and discipline, and there are destructive and sinful ways of life that we must not abide by. We cannot take advantage of God's grace and mercy and refuse to meditate on and correct the wrong things we do. But we equally cannot wallow in our misery, or drag the stones of our past into our future, or deny ourselves lives that are rich with the joy and blessing that Christ died to give us. I suppose we must rest in him more and practice being what he says we are—his children whom he loves more than we can imagine.

Your mistakes do not define you. Your past does not identify you. And neither do the good works you have done, or the eloquent sermons you have given, or the beautiful song you wrote, or the encouraging word you gave. In my own desert, I had to prepare a way for the Lord. I had to understand that he was making his way toward me to do his work in my life. Not because of anything good or bad in me but just because of who he is . . . love.

I've found that whenever I am grasping at straws to feel God's love, I am inspired to show someone kindness, or do something nice for someone, or be the kind of person I believe God wants me to be. It's usually for the type of person who is the hardest to do these sorts of things for. I am convinced this is one way healing comes and God reveals himself to us in ways that he could not have otherwise done. If we stopped harassing ourselves for five minutes and started thinking about someone else, we would catch a glimpse of love. We all need to do things like this more often.

Rise from the Dust

Thomas Merton said, "When the Lord hears my prayer for mercy (a prayer which is itself inspired by the action of His mercy), then He makes His mercy present and visible in me by moving me to have mercy on others as He has had mercy on me."[3]

When your eyes open to the freedom in experiencing God's love, it is easier to paint an exquisitely beautiful picture of God to someone else because you can relate to those who stand in your once-messed-up spiritual circumference. You feel their pain, and your heart breaks when you see a person who oozes suffering and angst through every flooded pore, someone you know who is really trying hard, someone with a cataclysmic life journey that you could have easily mirrored had it not been for reasons you still can't quite figure out.

Recently I received an unexpected phone call from a family member I was once very close to. As a matter of fact, she was my best friend growing up. We experienced similar familial environments and wore some of the same ugly scars. Because we both had the same amount of undue pressure to be and act and look like people we were clearly not created to be, we clung to one another in a love alliance. We were each other's rock. A haven. A safe place for acceptance and belonging. I'm sure in some sense we were codependent, but I still believe we truly needed each other so desperately at that time.

As we grew older, we were sorely separated by geographical distance, petty arguments, and unnecessary pride. Our disconnect, however, climaxed in a terrible way. In hindsight, I think we were both unable to reconcile our own insecurities and were in the prenatal stages of individual addictions. While I can't speak on her behalf, I can share what flowed from my own emotional instability.

She was skinny; I was chubby. She had beautiful hair; mine was limp and dull. She had a way with men; I had a way with books. She had a chunky bank account at her disposal; I was on the verge of bankruptcy. She basically got the kind of attention I never knew how to garner. These things sound so stupid, don't they? Keep in mind I was only twenty years old and my confidence evolved from a hodgepodge of self-destructive and meaningless things.

On a beautiful spring day we got into a verbal battle on her front porch. It escalated with fists. Hers flew, and after I strategically ducked two or three times, I trotted off toward my car mentally patting myself on the back for being the bigger person. I knew she was in earshot right before I slammed my car door, and I suddenly became intoxicated with the bitter juices of venom that dripped from my lips. I called her—among other things—crazy, a loser, psychotic, and a slut. All the things I knew she was so sensitive about. The names I knew she was called by those who were supposed to love and protect her.

Now, I am not giving this girl a free pass on instigating the fight or on being hurtful and irrational in her own way, but let me be clear that I was not just an innocent victim. Sure, I didn't bash the living snot out of her, but my blows were felt at a much deeper level—in a place where cuts, scrapes, and bruises have the ability to remain indefinitely.

We have never spoken more than a few words to each other since that time. When my grandmother died some-odd years ago, I approached this old friend during the funeral and made a peace offering. With all of my heart, I wanted to let go of the pains we had both purposefully exchanged and was willing to take the lead in creating a forgiving—or even just a kinder—place. She looked at me like I was crazy and walked away. Maybe I was crazy. I don't know.

Whenever I saw her at a family function after that, it was impossible for me to hide my unease. I felt uncomfortable when she was around. I wasn't afraid, by any means, but I could physically feel this haunting sense of hatred she had for me. There was no sense of normalcy in her voice. Her tone was flat and fake, and it was obvious I repulsed her. Even being in the same room with her made my skin crawl. So I avoided her at all costs.

A few weeks ago, she left me a message. She needed my help. It was a simple request, albeit unusual after basically ignoring me for eight years. She needed a ride to the vet because her new puppy was sick. She had lost her driver's license and nobody would drive her. She was sorry for all the stupid stuff that had happened. She forgave and forgot. And would I please help her out with this one favor?

I listened to the message, and after gaining composure from the initial blast of shock, I thought to myself, "Well, heck, of course! Why not?" My heart turned to a pile of sentimental mush, mainly because I had heard through the family gossip train that she was going through a rough time. I knew she was in the throes of doing some serious internal work. I knew she was still battling the same demons whose poisonous talons had left scars on my own shoulders. I knew she had a distorted image of true, God-inspired love. Because I had lived in such a similar place not too long ago, driving her ten minutes away was the least that I could do. But nothing could have prepared me for our rendezvous.

When she plopped down in my car and our eyes met, something happened that I can only describe as being from a spiritual realm. All my defenses and anxiety and judgments and feelings I had for her instantaneously vanished. I looked at her through what I believe were God's eyes. In that moment, I loved her with such an intense depth it was simply indescribable. It wasn't that I felt sorry for her, by any means; I genuinely loved her.

I was literally stunned as I watched her body begin to shake. It was the first time I had seen anybody have a full-fledged panic attack. As I drove to the vet's office, she talked nonstop and her hands shook with tremors. Tears flooded her pretty eyes. "Am I going to be okay? Look at me, I'm a wreck, right? I'm having a fit. I need to breathe. I'm sorry. Oh my God, I'm so scared."

Then she started to say things that made my heart break. "Do you think God still loves me? I read the Bible all the time. If I keep doing that, will he help me? What else should I do? Should I go to church? Oh my God, oh my God, I'm going to die. I am going to die, right? I just feel it. Does God still love me? Will he help me? He must hate me. I'm never going to get better."

I could hear the soundtrack of the terrible things people had said about her that had taken up permanent residence in her spirit. I could see the looming cloud of pain and self-torture that surrounded her heart like an impenetrable fortress. I also knew the terrible light she had pictured herself in was not the light God beamed in her direction. I related to the agony of living in a perpetual state of masochism from a life of making poor choices and bad decisions. I was so conscious of how, during that wretched time, the true image of God is blurred beyond recognition.

So, as corny as it may sound, I spoke truth into her life and verbally showered her with blessings. While I had nothing to give as far as sound, meaningful, or wise advice, I offered her words of health, success, spiritual fulfillment, love, truth, and above all else, the peace that passes understanding. We have never spoken since, but I make sure to pray for her every day.

This is not a story to reflect my good nature. It is a lesson I learned about the kind of God that I serve: that the overwhelming amount of love and goodness and compassion and mercy and hope I had for her in that moment—though sincere—was paltry compared to the love, goodness, compassion, mercy, and hope God has for her and for all of his children. We do not need to daily flog our backs with cat-o'-nine-tails; or constantly remind ourselves and God of our (in the words of my pastor) perpetual wretchedness; or rely on the superstitious act of tearing petals from a flower to determine whether or not God really loves us; or engage in what we think are holy acts just to redeem some measure of worth; or desperately dig our nails into his scarred feet, scratch our eyes out in agony, and leave his altar with raw and bleeding knees thinking that maybe, just maybe, this will make him love us more.

This reminds me of a verse in Isaiah: "Rise from the dust, O Jerusalem. Sit in a place of honor. Remove the chains of slavery from your neck, O captive daughter of Zion" (52:2 NLT). Oh, how we mercilessly bind ourselves with chains so the walk toward the throne of mercy is made nearly impossible. How we delight in drowning ourselves in dirty pools of guilt and shame. And how we foolishly trash our spirits with dung and mire instead of allowing grace to take shelter where it belongs.

Rise from the dust, O captive son and daughter of Zion. Rise from the dust.

2

CONFESSIONS OF AN IMPERFECT CHRISTIAN

Have no fear of perfection—you'll never reach it.

Salvador Dali

In my early twenties I dated a guy whose main goal in life was to be a balanced man. He did a pretty impressive job. To this day I don't think I have ever met a person as nearly perfectly symmetrical in different life areas as he was. Aaron said something to me once that, though I responded at the time by burning with rage, I have learned in time to appreciate: "We will never completely know another person, even in a long, lasting, and happy marriage, because it's simply impossible to know exactly what anybody is thinking."

I was startled and blurted out, "What? That's crazy!" Hearing him say that challenged my naive belief that once you found your "soul mate," you would learn everything about them and always know what they were thinking. You would share, if you will, a couples' ESP because that simply was a key perk of experiencing true love. During the dialogue that followed, I started to wonder what exactly were some of the things in Aaron's mind that I wouldn't be privy to. What dirty secrets was he hiding? What perverse thoughts surged through his brain? Was he saying one thing and thinking the complete opposite? Was he pretending to like me but really trying to figure out the most painless way to break up with me?

For a long time Aaron's remark made me feel uneasy about trusting people, particularly those with whom I shared an intimate relationship. I wanted to count on the credo that it was possible to know the people you were close to, whether husbands, boyfriends, sisters, or best friends, like you know the back of your hand; it was just too frightening to consider the type of unimaginable evil or lies that cluttered the inner lives of those I loved. I soon hyperpersonalized this concept and started to believe that no person was being altogether genuine with me.

Somewhere down the road I crawled out of my infantine cave and stopped thinking about people's inner sanctum as a place for them to use, manipulate, or trick me. I saw the statement for exactly what it was and came to the basic and fundamental conclusion that we all possess thoughts, feelings, and ideas that we don't want, or maybe don't even need, to share with anyone else. Let me start by saying that I believe in the general good of people. I tend to give most the benefit of the doubt and don't typically judge people by a negative isolated incident or a rough patch they happen to be going through.

That being said, I am very much acquainted with human nature at its best and at its worst, or just in its being. I understand that all of us think and feel things that may not be kosher. Maybe someone we are talking to really annoys us. Maybe we'd prefer to be working out instead of helping our mother fertilize her garden. Maybe we'd rather be at the beach than sitting in church on a holiday weekend. On a deeper level, maybe we even wonder what it would be like to kiss our married co-worker. Maybe we are so incredibly stressed, overworked, and drained that we wish we could have twenty-four hours where we didn't have to think or remember but instead could experience hedonistic pleasure, the type where anything goes.

Honesty is the best policy? Maybe, maybe not. If I ask you if you think I'm a talented writer and you start hemming and hawing—another way of saying no—then I'd rather you not tell me the truth, as I'm much too insecure. But honesty is certainly the best policy as it concerns ourselves. I think if we were all intentional about telling ourselves the truth of what lies inside of us—even in those deep, dark, and hidden corners of our soul—we would save ourselves much trouble down the road. We would nip future problems closer to the bud. We would stop living life as fake and seemingly perfect people. We would strengthen our spiritual walk.

I want to talk about being authentic as we trudge, saunter, or dance down the path of faith. A lot of us are quite adept at molding our exterior shells and demeanors so we give off an air of at least near perfection. We don't do the obvious bad stuff, like swear, drink, smoke, or have premarital sex. We also act responsibly at all times, we say and do the right things, and we generally fall comfortably into the proverbial box that society, our family, our church, or our spouse has created for us. We don't rock the boat. Our rhetoric is always upbeat, and our emotions are fixed regardless of variables.

Step outside of yourself for a minute. I want you to examine the superficial web that you have so delicately and artfully weaved around your spotless life. Tell the truth. Who pushes your buttons? What frustrates you? What kind of white lies do you tell? What are you tempted with that you would have never even thought you were capable of doing? What would you do if there was no chance you would get caught? Before we can be honest with others and even with God, we have to privately gauge the truth of who we are. Or what we are feeling. Or what we are thinking about. Jim Davis said, "The truth will set you free, but first it will make you miserable." He was right.

Some-odd years ago I found myself liking a married man, who had a successful career in the music industry, in a not-purely-platonic sort of way. The feelings were mutual. Neither of us ever acted on any sexual impulse, primarily because we both had too much to risk. Make no mistake: something illicit, however unripe, was brewing. In the beginning I found myself purposely ignoring the signs of attraction—the way our touch lingered just a little longer than necessary; the way our eyes orchestrated knowing, wanting gazes; the way our bodies were hypnotically drawn to each other, if only just to delicately graze each others' skin as if by accident.

I did my Christian duty, or so I thought, and pretended a connection did not exist. I beat my brain silly trying to believe that I could never even have these sorts of feelings for this man or any married man. I was a good girl, after all. I knew very well the possible troubles associated with playing with fire. I knew not to engage in flirty or too-friendly behavior that might spark suggestive energy to an unavailable man. But eventually I caved in and recognized the truth that a messy situation had probably started to hatch.

This happened after a chat I had with a good friend I had known for many years. Though I loved her dearly and held her in high esteem, I always suspected she suffered from an acute form of naïveté. At least I thought of her as too naive to talk openly and honestly about issues buried deep beneath superficial surfaces. This frequently led me to avoid controversial topics or matters of the darker heart. But for some reason or another this woman, who had been happily married for ten years and had what most consider a perfect life, manipulated the conversation to the topic of extramarital affairs. I don't know if it was for her benefit, or a God-thing for mine (nobody knew how I felt about this man), or just meaningless happenstance, but when I hung up the phone, something had stirred in my spirit.

"I can see how people can have affairs," she remarked matter-of-factly. "Sometimes you just want to feel sexy, like a woman, for goodness' sake, and if you're not getting that kind of attention from your husband or anyone else, well, I can see how you would want to get that attention somewhere else."

My ears perked. This was getting juicy. I offered, "You know, we can all find other people more attractive than our special someone. That's a fact. And if we're hanging out with someone in a platonic way who even a little bit tickles our fancy, it just takes that one crappy day when we feel so frustrated for us to either accept or make the next move. The one day you get into a big fight with your husband, or if your wife says or does something incredibly stupid or hurtful, or if you're single and the loneliness gets too overwhelming and you have a real terrible day at the office, then *wham!* You start exploring the world of infidelity. Out of nowhere—but not really. It's been there all along; we just ignore it until one day comes and blows it all up."

"Yup," my friend agreed. "Just one bad day and all the feelings you have hidden about the affair you swore you'd never have come out, and before you know it, you're doing some hanky-panky. Even I'll admit that."

In that space of honesty, I realized my awful truth. I could have an affair. I really could. I was feeding off the bewitching lure of seduction. Not only that, but the fact was, I was really attracted to this man, and not just on a physical level. I liked being around him. He made me feel good. He made me get all warm and tingly. Whenever I was around him I felt like a "woman."

Being single for what seemed like forever and having the opposite of a *Sex and the City* dating life, a part of my sexuality was so dormant I wondered if it even existed. I genuinely questioned whether or not I was attractive, sexy, or ever considered an object of desire to the opposite sex, because I really had nothing to tell or show me that I was. And here was this creatively brilliant and extraordinarily talented married man who was kindling the sexual magnetism I hoped was still there.

When my friend and I ended our talk, I finally unveiled this telling truth to myself—the truth that even I didn't want to believe about myself. The reality was that if the stars were aligned, if I was feeling especially solitary, if I felt kicked and dragged by a disturbing life event, if I was certain no one was around, it could happen. I could become a contributing factor in destroying a marital vow. This petrified me.

My prayers, as a result, became nothing short of blubbering messes. I purged the intricacies of what was happening inside of me in an unrelenting and desperate way. It wasn't fair I was plagued by loneliness. It wasn't fair that I was still alone. It wasn't fair that others could have their cake and eat it too. It wasn't fair that I was a hot-blooded, vivacious blonde who had to suppress herself from what seemed only natural. It wasn't fair that this man made my knees weak.

Albert Einstein, among his many other brilliant thoughts, once said, "The search for truth implies a duty. One must not conceal any part of what one has recognized to be true." Once I got honest with myself and then with God, I felt a sense of responsibility. The truth was out, though kept between him and me, and I had to do something about it. I needed to exercise caution, discipline, and wisdom and graciously step out of this sexual limelight I wanted so badly to bask in.

Needless to say, it was an excruciating process. I'd be a liar if I told you that the feelings vanished overnight or that the next day I looked at him with as much empty attraction as I would feel toward my brother or someone who looked like Pee-wee Herman. The feelings slowly dissipated, dreadfully sluggishly, I'm afraid. My only remedy during this painful time was to offer my honesty in prayer and recite the words—as in one of Anne Lamott's favorite prayers—"Help me, help me, help me."[1]

Many people look at me and assume that because I'm naturally bubbly, optimistic, good-natured, sweet, kind, and compassionate, nothing to the contrary exists inside of my heart. That I have no unsanitary thoughts, that I am pure in all corners, and that only innocence pours from my being. Now, I am not an evil hellion, by any means, and I don't depict an image that is antithetical to who I really am in my character. I assure you I am not a fake, but I am certainly not perfect and don't claim to be.

You would be surprised at some of the stuff that I think about. But before you start pointing accusatory fingers at me or become so greedy in wanting to find out what those things are, stop and take a look at yourself. Take stock of your own inner mind and heart. Think about the unholy messes that tap-dance around your spirit. Think about the haunting demons that you wish would go away. Are you perfect? Almost perfect? Righteous? Holy? An ideal example of a believer?

It takes a lot of guts to be honest with yourself and wash away the greasy layers of false perfection you have slathered on your skin.

It is humbling to look in the mirror and verbalize what is going on inside that you don't want to even admit and would be mortified if people only knew. I don't think we have to beat ourselves over the head with what is sometimes the ugly reality of who we are, what we are thinking, or what lies deep within our hearts, but we have a call to be honest and to live our lives in faith authentically. And we do have a duty to carry it all to God in prayer. Don't worry; he won't pretend to be surprised.

Some of us need to move out of our glass houses. Don't think your brain will only be saturated by holy thoughts and the only desires you will ever experience will be to read the Bible and fast. Don't think that your impure thoughts can instantly vanish every time you simply utter the name of Jesus. Don't think that you are ever immune from saying, thinking, or doing something that you always thought you'd never do. We need grace, and we need Christ working in us at all times. Only through this honesty and asking for his help will we ever take care of the messes that plague some of us. Nothing of our own doing will help us be better people; that comes only through Christ himself. As Heini Arnold said, "We are not so self-controlled or exert sharp will power because of how great we are. As long as we think we can save ourselves by our own will power, we will only make the evil in us stronger than ever." It's simple. We all need Jesus.

Screw-Ups and Stumbles

A televangelist falls from grace as proof of adulterous affairs leaks out. He has been fooling around with young men right under the nose of his unsuspecting wife.

A prominent conservative politician is caught smoking something to keep his energy up. He is ratted out by his drug dealer.

A pastor's wife reaches a breaking point and viciously slaughters her husband with a steak knife she got as a wedding gift five years ago. She says she was depressed and that he beat her. How do you feel when you read or see stories like these in a newspaper or on television? It's shocking and embarrassing, isn't it? I know it makes people, especially those of the same faith, cringe because these self-declared Christians are supposed to be making headlines of a more positive nature. They should be commended for creating soup kitchens in poverty-stricken communities, or for raising millions of dollars for global hunger relief efforts, or for celebrating fifty years of happy marriage. Instead, they are publicly humiliated after being found out.

Some people of no faith find these exposés incredibly gratifying. They get a kick out of seeing believers fall flat on their faces because they consider it discrediting to faith. If people who claim to be Christ-followers have the capacity to screw up in such royal fashion, why believe? Why pray to a God who can't even make us skip down the straight and narrow path with ease and relative comfort? Why even strive to follow lofty standards if they are impossible to attain?

These illustrations may seem to represent a severe form of imperfect Christian, but I use them because recently our headlines seem inundated with similar ones. This should sober us fellow believers to the reality of what can make someone go from personifying faith and morality to screwing up in a royal sense. I don't condone immoral, unethical, violent, or illegal behavior by Christians. I don't sugarcoat the issue by saying, "Oh well, nobody is perfect." Know that such behavior repulses me and I think there should be, and usually are, pretty severe repercussions. But neither am I bowled over when I hear real-life accounts of decent, faith-believing people who seem nice, quiet, and normal doing something atrocious that reflects the total opposite of their supposed good nature.

It makes my heart break and reminds me of our general human frailties—that none of us, the believer and nonbeliever alike, is immune to destructive thoughts, behaviors, or actions and that unless we are really careful with how we conduct our internal lives, we are all capable of even the most unimaginable evil. I'm also careful not to find pleasure in seeing someone caught with their pants down (no pun intended). Caught—that's an interesting notion, isn't it? Some of us have wisely stopped our troubling behaviors or activities before anyone had the chance to witness our fall. And, let's admit it, others of us have been caught with our hand in some kind of cookie jar at some point in our lives.

We should never forget that human beings are human beings regardless of who their family is, how often they work out, where they were born, what church they attend, how many times they weep through Wednesday night prayer meetings, or what their political affiliation is. Unless we are in constant communion with God, unless we are allowing him to regularly search our hearts and our thoughts, unless we have people in our lives who are not afraid to lovingly call us out on our questionable activities or thought processes, we can do some pretty horrible things. Some of us are, of course, more inclined to do particular things. Joe may have more of a tendency to overindulge in alcohol. Suzy may have more of a tough time not sleeping around. Andrew may be more challenged in the area of pride. Rachel may be more apt to overspend to make herself feel better. Yet at the end of the day, we must not forget that we are all capable of slipping, falling, stumbling, and outright falling flat on our faces. All of us. Your neighbor. Your boss. Your pastor. Him. Her. You. Me.

Christians have to be very wise in how we conduct ourselves because we are taught to live under a moral code and with high standards. That's a fact. Let's put the grave immoral, illegal, and outright spiritually rebellious acts aside right now and talk about our example of faith in the context of gray issues, or what my pastor calls "disputable matters"—items regarding which the Bible does not provide a black-and-white answer for what we should or should not do. Should we drink alcohol? Is smoking bad? What about uttering a curse word when we get a flat tire on a deserted highway at three in the morning?

We all have our opinions, biblically based or otherwise, on what we consider to be a "perfect" Christian. Many believers define the perfect Christian by what we do, what we wear, what we listen to, what we watch, what we read, what we appreciate, and so on. And if what we have determined as un-Christian behavior is visible in someone else, we judge, we point fingers, and we become frustrated and disappointed with their "unholy" behavior.

Do Christians make mistakes? Do we experience temptation? Do we do stupid things? Do we act first and think later? Sure. We are not immune to bad and foolish behavior. So what is the perfect Christian? Well, no one is perfect, for one thing, so let me get rid of that word. What makes a *true* Christian might be a better question to address. I think it is someone who is in relationship with God and who is continually maturing in their faith. Someone who is honest about themselves, recognizing frailties and weakness and understanding that it is only by the grace of God that we are deemed good. Someone who desperately sees a need to be daily or even hourly renewed in mind and spirit. Someone who is genuinely "working out" their salvation (Phil. 2:12) and is not afraid to be corrected yet is not pigeonholed by others and their ideas of holiness.

When Religion Gets in the Way

In my own life, I have been so bothered by religious people who substantiate the faith of others by what they perceive as the image a believer should emulate. There are, for instance, way too many seemingly perfect believers who live in tiny, closed-lid boxes. They are so inundated with Christian culture that they forget they live in a pretty huge world filled with people of different ethnicities, vocations, cultural customs, spiritual beliefs, political views, and so on. Anything they consider non-Christian is outright sinful. I just don't relate well to that type of thinking. I find myself purposefully disassociating myself from people like this because I find them incredibly naive, close-minded, and highly subject to premature and even wrong judgment.

When I lived in the Bible Belt, I attended a church where everyone thought the same things, joined the same clubs, and read the same books, and many of them even looked the same. As a matter of fact, a good 80 percent of the young people in that congregation were leaders in ministry at a local college. There is nothing wrong with being a campus leader, but they almost frowned upon people who held secular jobs. Why settle for an occupation in finance when you could save souls forty hours a week? I must say they did like people who had prominent executive jobs, mainly because their paychecks could support the campus leaders. But everyone else in between? Big deal.

I got the sense, from the many conversations I listened to, that they felt balanced spirituality was almost boring and pointless. More often than not, they emphasized the supernatural part of religion. You were pretty holy, for example, or clearly worthy of special attention from God, if you were slain in the Spirit, or rolled around on the floor speaking in tongues for three hours, or had visions in the middle of grocery shopping, or heard God's voice telling you the best way to tie your shoes.

One such young lady was so "unworldly" that you had to be so careful what you said or what opinions you shared around her. She was the type whom God told everything to, from who she should date to which coffee shop she should go to. She spoke very quietly and gently and had huge brown eyes that would unnaturally widen when she started talking about her faith. It wasn't a sweet expression, mind you; she looked bugged out. If you mentioned a spiritual issue you were struggling with or questioned, without fail she would lean in real close to you, cock her head, and expand her peepers. I'm sure she was trying to show she was interested in what you were saying, but really it looked kind of weird. Almost like she was trying to prove how attentive she was to your desperate or heathen cause.

We had a discussion once about faith and doubt. I am a firm believer that they can coexist. She said I was wrong. Differences of opinions are normal, sure, but she approached my thoughts in a patronizing, condescending way and ended our talk by saying she would pray for me. Hey, I need prayer like the next guy on the street, but she acted like I was the antithesis of a believer and so needed prayer to save me from the pits of hell. I just wanted to offer my beliefs to a listening ear, but she used it as an opportunity to set me straight and to force-feed me her mumbo-jumbo, Christianese ideologies. It didn't help; it made me want to throw up. Actually, it made me want to shake her around a bit, but as a Christian myself, that would have been out of the question. I don't want to create the perception that I didn't think she was a nice person. It's just that she was annoying (there, I said it) and the kind of faith she touted made me want to run in the opposite direction.

To be fair, maybe I was being somewhat sensitive. I was definitely in a delicate place in my spiritual walk, as at that time I found myself miserably bored and even irritated with Christianity. I was really looking to find a healthy balance of being a Christian integrated in a capacious world and experiencing the joy and freedom of faith without feeling the dire need to preach to every person I came in contact with and slap "My boss is a Jewish carpenter" bumper stickers on my car. I didn't want to be a Christian who lived with my head in the clouds and believed the only meaningful purpose in life was to convince people to "turn or burn." I wanted to be, well, normal. Balanced. Christlike without having to give up or change my God-given effervescent personality. I didn't want to be boring or make it my mission to be viewed as "holy" or untouchable. I wanted to be me. A me who loved Jesus and was open to him repairing whatever needed to be fixed in my spirit.

I'm sorry, but many holy rollers who have Holy Ghost experiences every three seconds kill religion, especially the Christian faith. I'm not saying we should be crackheads or hookers or corporate swindlers for Jesus. But we should be ourselves without feeling the need to look, act, and sound like the perfect Christian who has it all together all of the time.

In my anti-church days I woke up one Sunday and had an indescribable urge to visit a house of worship. I took a trip to some church, the name of which I can't even remember now, and slipped incognito into one of the back pews. During the announcements, an attractive blonde woman who could have easily passed for Kim Cattrall literally plopped down beside me. She gave me an incredibly warm and inviting smile that sent chills down my spine.

I noticed she was sitting rather slouched down and kept clutching her stomach. She noticed I noticed and flashed me a million-dollar smile with a twinkle in her eye. "I have the absolute worst cramps ever. And my kids acted up this morning like you wouldn't believe. It's a miracle I'm here, I tell you, a miracle." In our three-minute gab session—during the special song someone sang—I found out she was the wife of one of the pastors. She told me how great it was that I was in church and that I should definitely come back. She even gave me one of those new-people-at-church cards to fill out if I felt comfortable doing so.

I felt so welcomed by her without feeling like a backslider or sinner. What was it about her that made me experience this comfort? She was delightful in the most authentic way. She threw me off guard with her natural essence. As odd as it may sound, she showed a refreshing type of honesty in admitting her achy abdomen and the morning rush challenge she'd had with her feisty young kids. The vibe she gave off wasn't sickly sugarcoated. She was real. That is the type of Christian that I like and that I relate to.

I know it was a short conversation, but it was her demeanor that brought me back to the church the next Sunday. I think we could all learn a thing or two from that.

When I Don't Feel Like a Christian

I feel less than classy drinking expensive French wine in a white Styrofoam coffee cup with the words *LaVazza—Italy's favorite coffee* blazoned on it in bold, blue letters. Especially in the afternoon. But I'm on vacation and I'm not allowed to bring glass on the beach. Classless or not, I tell you, I feel wonderful. At ease. Like everything is going to be all right. I haven't felt this way in a long time. (It's not the wine, I assure you; I've only had three sips.)

Now I'm staring at a turquoise sea so luminescent it seems to have a layer of Swarovski crystals topping the wispy ripples of gentle waves. The sun is brilliant, and the small handful of sun worshipers around me seem to be talking in airy whispers so as not to be an audible distraction from the natural beauty surrounding them. I tell you again, I feel calm. Peaceful. Good. Light.

This lasts only for a few minutes before the guilt starts to pour in: the guilt over what Christians are supposed to feel like or how they are supposed to spend their time or what is supposed to attract their fancy.

For instance, perhaps I should have spent the summer feeding the poor in Calcutta instead of feverishly trying to meet all my work deadlines. Perhaps I should be proselytizing my faith to the elderly couple sitting next to me listening to Chubby Checker. Maybe I should grab Jesus's hand and introduce him to Scott, the cabana boy who gets me fresh towels more often than is probably reasonably necessary. Yesterday was Sunday; maybe I should have found a church on the island to attend. Should I have worn a bikini with the words "Property of God" in fluorescent letters?

These are the thoughts that pop into my head that make me feel, well, un-Christian. Unholy. The opposite of the apostle Paul in chains in prison singing worship songs. I'm getting better at not allowing random guilt-ridden and erratic feelings to ultimately dominate or suppress me. I'm definitely becoming an expert at wielding my sword to chase away these debilitating notions, mostly with God's help. These thoughts are certainly not effective barometers for measuring the depth of spirituality; they are, for the most part, stupid.

Once I close my eyes and ask God if there is any truth to them, I am enveloped by an overwhelming sense of calm. It's not the physical sentiment of feeling giddy or the knot-in-the-stomach feeling of fear; it's an overall peace. Like a nothingness in the best sense of the word. I feel like I am exactly where I should be right now. I don't need to trumpet my faith by jumping up and down and waving my hands around like a toddler who just ate five Snickers bars. I rest in the peace that passes understanding, the peace that passes even the feelings and thoughts that serve us no ultimate good. I need to have these kinds of moments more often.

We all have days when we feel unspiritual. I don't mean feeling spiritually off-kilter when we engage in behaviors or acts that are clearly immoral; I'm talking about the times when you just feel blah, indifferent, tired, or annoyed. When your kids have obnoxious attitudes the size of continents. Or when you are so busy at your job that you can't remember what day of the week it is. Or when you feel so burdened by something that it crushes your ability to function at a relatively normal level. I don't know anyone who feels super Christian all the time. Actually, I take that back. I do, and I think they're weird and have an unhealthy and warped sense of reality.

My sister Vivien is on a spiritual journey, and every now and again she calls me to ask, "Do you ever not feel spiritual?" She knows the answer but will faithfully ask because it can be quite a troubling sentiment to experience. We think maybe we're doing something wrong. Maybe we're on the wrong path. Maybe God is mad at us. Maybe we've even imagined this whole faith thing.

The reality of my life is that I have my unique moods and moments. I'm not a holy roller who thinks ethereal or chaste thoughts twenty-four hours a day. I get indignant sometimes when people who work in customer service are rude to me. People who are emotionally flat and never share their true feelings irritate me. I sometimes have a tendency to act first and think later. I probably spend too much money. Some days I even sulk, and my attitude is wretched. Being around people can make my skin crawl.

Sometimes even the gurgling coos of an infant make me want to shush her because, for Pete's sake, "I can't even think!"

I don't just have bad attitudes here and there. I have my good moments too. I have meaningful conversations with the cleaning people because I know there is more to them than being called "cleaning people." They have lives and families and joys and troubles that many do not regard simply because they are scrubbing our toilets. I come to a screeching halt in the middle of a grueling run in a park because the beauty is so overwhelming it brings tears to my eyes. I can't help but fall to my knees and worship the Creator in response to his magnificent and perfect design of nature. My heart dances out of sheer joy when a friend I've been praying for calls me and tells me something that I can only attribute to divine intervention, to the answering of prayer.

"But people annoy you," you say. "Babies irritate you." "You act on impulse." Yeah, yeah, yeah. I'm working on these things. Let's not forget that. I constantly pray for God to work through me to make me a better person. It's the ultimate self-development program. I'm a work in progress—we've all heard that. I think we have this idea, though, that after one day or a week or ninety days, we will have reached ultimate patience, goodness, and charity. Please. We are *continual* works in progress. My internal work is better than last year, but I've still got a lot of stuff I need to develop. I have both good and bad moments. If you are looking for a perfect witness of faith to shine in righteous glory and say the right things all of the time and not be honest about who I am or what I think, for heaven's sake, stop reading this book.

I have somehow created this image in my head of what a Christian should think about, feel, and be like, and whenever I hold myself up in comparison, I fail miserably. I come up short on every end imaginable. I am learning, in many challenging ways, how to

CONFESSIONS OF AN IMPERFECT CHRISTIAN

be myself, how to not compromise what God has created me to be, and how to live by his example.

Martin Luther said, "This life, therefore, is not righteousness, but growth in righteousness; not health, but healing; not being, but becoming; not rest, but exercise. We are not yet what we shall be, but we are growing toward it. The process is not yet finished, but it is going on. This is not the end, but it is the road. All does not yet gleam in glory, but all is being purified."[2] Confessions of an imperfect Christian? I'm a Jesus-follower, I love him with all my heart, and I have my good and bad stretches. As you journey on the road of faith, know that all sorts of times will come. Good ones, bad ones, tempting ones, peaceful ones, trying ones, carefree ones, sobering ones, and funny ones. Just be honest about them; tell the truth, especially to yourself and to God. Being honest is really the only tool that will develop your spirituality. Truth may not be pretty or classy or perfect, but know that as you are "working out" your faith, he is working in you. That is our hope.

3

CONVERSATIONS WITH GOD

Prayer is not asking. It is a longing of the soul.

Mahatma Gandhi

I am an advocate of prayer. Prayer is important. Whether you are a seasoned Christian or you feel spiritually destitute. Whether every facet of your life is fine and dandy or the bomb shelters you have so carefully constructed are crumbling right before your very eyes. For me, the most important purpose of prayer is simply to deliberately create an opportunity to commune with God. To sit with him in honesty. To behold the eternal scars that adorn his hands and feet. To rest in his presence. To get to know him.

I was in Las Vegas some time ago during a time in my life when I was sweeping up the million broken pieces of the messes I had made from bad decisions, foolish choices, heartbreak, addiction, and happenstance. My uncle Steve had invited me on this trip with his two delightful kids so I could babysit them. I was happy to oblige. My cousins are amazing, and they make me smile and relax in the presence of their giggles, wonder, and innocence.

One morning I couldn't sleep. I was miserable and depressed thinking about a plethora of little things that weighed about as much as a Navy battleship on my mind. I felt scared. Nervous. Even almost absent of faith. A few hours later, I was sitting at the pool with Uncle Steve, and as he does on so many occasions I can't even begin to count, he voiced one of his inspiring monologues about faith, God, and the spiritual path. He stressed the importance of spending time with God (yes, even on vacation in Las Vegas) and shoved one of Joel Osteen's devotional pamphlets in my sunburned face to read. I was kind of embarrassed because he was talking really loudly and I thought the last thing people needed to hear on vacation in the sweltering heat was a sermon on faith. I wanted to cover their ears so they could drink their piña coladas and frolic in the pool in peace.

A part of me groaned and humored Uncle Steve by paying partial attention to what he was saying—only partial because I already knew the gist of what he was trying to convey. "Tell me something I don't know," I silently begged. "Tell me something more exciting, more profound, more concrete. Tell me my life is going to be okay and everything is going to work out because God told you to tell me. Give me the answers of what I'm supposed to do and where I'm supposed to be. And please, for Pete's sake, show me the blueprint of exactly how everything is going to work out, inch by inch, line by line." Still, another part of me hung on his every word. I was anxious to find a lightbulb epiphany somewhere in the verbiage that boisterously shot out of his mouth.

As I grasped the devotional in my hand and darted my eyes toward the juicy fiction book I was already reading, I promised myself that by the time the sun set, I would flip through the devotional. Then I exchanged Joel Osteen for my juicy fiction book and tossed the pamphlet under my lounge chair. But I was unable to ignore an uncanny gnawing in my spirit, and five minutes later there I was, meditating on each positive message this smiling megachurch pastor had written. I couldn't take my eyes off one of the titles: "Feed Your Faith." I felt nudged by something outside of myself. I can't give you a verbatim account of what I believed God was saying to me at the time, but it went something like this: "Pray more. Spend more time with me. This is how you feed your faith."

For a few weeks after the Sin City trip, I couldn't get these thoughts out of my head. They consumed me. Every day I woke up, made myself a cup of coffee, and plunged headfirst into my work, but the pressing suggestion of "Spend time with me" made it almost impossible for me to think or do anything else. Finally I obliged and made a commitment to begin every day—as I had done off and on in the course of my existence—with prayer.

Colossians 4:2 reminds us to devote ourselves to prayer, and this is a great thing to do, primarily to maintain the spiritual and mysterious connection between human being and divine being. But let's get real. The commitment to prayer is sometimes viewed as such an exciting task as raking leaves or getting your teeth cleaned. To some of us it seems more like drudgery than opportunity. Many hail the great excuse that we are too busy to pray. With great frustration and annoyance, we present God with the myriad of stuff that devours our time—our spouses, our kids, our jobs, our hobbies, our legal troubles, the deadlines we are frantically trying to meet, the many commitments we have vowed to uphold, and the sick family members we are caring for. Like expert attorneys, we make the case that we don't have the time or the energy to pray and ask that in light of the roaring sea of odds and ends flooding our lives, would he please give us a well-deserved break in this area?

Bill Hybels wrote a book titled *Too Busy Not to Pray*. Not only is that a killer title, but it makes an incredibly revealing point. Sure, all of us are swamped by life events and responsibilities, but we are all too busy *not* to pray! I know for me, if I don't begin my day with some sort of spiritual connection, I feel off-kilter. I am more apt to run around my schedule and to-do lists like a chicken with its head cut off. I am more inclined to forget my inborn need for God. I am more likely to be anxious than peaceful, desperate than content, worried than restful. So I pray. Even when I don't feel like it.

I believe in the power of prayers containing language that is eloquent and articulate or colored with words that are, at best, messy examples of stutters and stammers. I'll be honest. The latter is probably more illustrative of my kinds of prayers. They tend to take on more of a conversational tone than a fluent script. I don't know why that is, and I used to harbor an extraordinary amount of guilt because of it. Don't think I am not respectful of God or am irreverent on purpose. Far from it. I think I just pray better in my own sputtering way. Quite frankly, I don't naturally have great oratorical skills, so I don't know why I ever imagined my prayers would be smooth spoken.

I know many people who pray almost poetically. The words flow effortlessly, there is never an extra "um" to ruin the moment, and they don't use "Dear Lord" in excess. They pray beautifully, and it makes me somewhat jealous. This is the reason I used to be afraid of prayer and am only now overcoming my fear of praying in public. My faith is present. My sincerity is present. My longing for God is present. But for some reason the words don't quite come out very pretty.

If I commit my personal unpardonable sin of listening to my speech, I tend to get discouraged. It sounds like a muttering mess.

My words are irritating, and they sound redundant. My brother and his wife took their kids to Disney World recently. He and his two-year-old son got stuck on the popular boat ride "It's a Small World" for about thirty minutes due to equipment failure. During that time, the tune replayed over and over and over again, competing against the cacophony of whiny complaints from adults and the shrill cries of toddlers. My nephew couldn't have been happier. With remarkable enthusiasm and not-quite-perfect pitch, he sang along each of the twenty or so times the song repeated. My brother, however, ever the calm, cool, and collected one, was a minute away from pulling his hair out. And one of the loudspeakers blaring "It's a Small World" was positioned right by his ear, which didn't help matters much. My brother now hates hearing that song. This is how I feel sometimes about my meditative monologues with the Almighty. It's a rhythmic blah, blah, blah, blah, blah without a choir of kids in the background and a keyboard accompaniment.

Not only that, but many times it takes a lot of effort to quiet myself, sit still, and prepare for my time of prayer. I get antsy. I think about doing laundry or that my facial skin feels dry or about how much money I've spent in the past two weeks on stupid things. Sometimes I even wonder if God is listening, if he cares, or if my words really do rise above the temporal world into his spiritual dimension. If I'm having trouble concentrating, I frequently feel the need to pinch myself and yell "Shhh!" in an attempt to refocus my attention on what I'm trying to say or, more importantly, to shift my thoughts to who it is I am praying to.

I heard Brennan Manning speak at a small, intimate conference many years ago. He discussed spending time with God and the simultaneous conflict of the human mind in thinking about things other than prayer. He said something like, "Some of us pray and all we're thinking about is eating McDonald's for lunch." I laughed nervously but was secretly ecstatic that I wasn't the only loser with selective ADD. He continued to expound on the guilt that we feel when our time with God doesn't look so neat and packaged, and he offered that that was okay. He suggested that God is just happy, beaming from holy ear to holy ear, that we're spending time with him. He sees our hearts, he sees our efforts, and he sees our willingness to want to commune with him. Hearing this former Franciscan priest say those things made me feel tons better and actually encouraged me, on so many different levels, to keep on praying, whatever it happens to sound like and however distracted I may be.

When I was going through a rough patch, I used to pray while smoking. I prayed while drinking. I prayed after one-night stands. I prayed because I was desperate for God to hear me. As bedraggled as I looked and felt, I yearned for him to change me, to fix me, to love me, to hug me, and to tell me everything was going to be okay. This is why I especially cheer people to pray when they feel so far from God—because uttering honesty in the midst of struggle or tragedy or our empty hollow selves reminds us and God of how much we need him. Maybe one day my prayers will be seasoned with perfect-sounding verbiage. In the meantime, I'm going to keep on praying and, like Brennan said, keep believing that God hears me in my tangled web of words and is really delighted that I've opted to spend time with him instead of doing God knows what.

A beautiful hymn written by Joseph Hart contains the following words:

> I will arise and go to Jesus
> He will embrace me in His arms.
> In the arms of my dear Savior
> O there are ten thousand charms.[1]

Wake up and sit in the quiet before him. And as much as you let him listen to you, listen to him. Embrace the tender moment that you are so lucky to have with a God who created the universe and longs to spend time with you. Interacting with him keeps us spiritually hooked up. It maintains our awareness with forces outside of ourselves. And it does feed our faith.

Wants, Needs, Answers, Miracles, and the Lack Thereof

You are probably looking for an answer to prayer. Maybe even a radical miracle. I am too. I believe in prayer because of the Source. I believe some answers to prayers come and others don't. All my love for and faith in prayers aside, at times I experience some tension. The reason is simple: I want my answers to prayer and miracles pretty badly. I want wisdom. I want that writing job. I want my church to grow. I want my friend's uncle's cancer to disappear. I want. I want. I want.

But I think about the girl I read about in the paper this morning, the tiny five-year-old dying of leukemia, and I am convinced she deserves a miracle more than I do. I think about the man who just came home from Iraq who lost both of his legs and, well, I just feel stupid asking God for whatever it is I'm asking for. I think about all the people who are praying for things like the victims of natural disasters, global warming, the poor, the sick, and victims of genocidal wars. I imagine the millions of saints out there with raw, bleeding knees and hoarse voices from their grave prayers. And I feel narcissistic. Vain. Selfish. It makes me want to crawl under a rock.

Yet the Bible tells us to pray. Whether or not we feel like it. Whether or not we need any answers at all. Whether or not we feel we deserve a holy operator on the other end who will do more than just place us on hold and subject us to elevator music. The Scriptures are filled with such inspiring petitions: "Do not be anxious about anything, but in everything, by prayer and petition, with thanksgiving, present your requests to God" (Phil. 4:6). "Pray . . . on all occasions" (Eph. 6:18). "Pray continually" (1 Thess. 5:17).

Why are we praying? What are we praying for? You pray for a wife. Your neighbor prays for deliverance. A mother prays for her kids' safety. A son prays for his father. A lawyer prays for victory. An actress prays for a gold statue. A sinner prays for salvation. A felon prays for grace. Should we feel guilty because we're praying, hoping for, and even at the height of belief *expecting* answers? Should we only pray for the big stuff, because God may not care about the small prayer requests that may seem trivial? Do you ever pray for stuff that seems, in the grand scheme of things, unimportant or insignificant?

About five years ago, I had to get rid of my beloved Rottweiler named Alta. My friends made fun of me because the year Alta came into my life was the year I prayed to fall in love. And I did . . . with a one-hundred-pound, gentle giant with the prettiest face in the universe, who loved chocolate chip cookies and who got incredibly excited when she saw bears on the National Geographic Channel. I'm going to go so far as to say that she was a literal Godsend. She burst into my life so unexpectedly and with such an incredible force, I think because God told her, "Alta, A. J. needs you right now, so I'm going to send you to her to take care of her. Be loving, be kind, be playful, and be good. Don't pee on the carpet. Don't jump up on visitors in her home. Don't shed too much. Don't bark at weird hours of the night. Just love her."

Alta attacked another dog one day at my apartment complex. She thought I felt threatened by this dog and pounced on the poor animal. It took four adults to pry my dog off of the other dog, who wasn't injured except for a nick on its ear that didn't even require stitches. When management got wind of what had happened, they freaked out and told me—appropriately so in hindsight, though at the time it made me want to wring their necks—that she had to be out of my house in ten days. Actually, they initially said three, but when they realized how upset I was, they tacked on another seven days to calm me down.

I didn't leave my bed for two whole days. No joke. I held Alta in my arms and cried and cried and cried. I was beyond distraught. When I barely lapsed out of my mini-depression, just enough to start making some phone calls to see what options I had, I soon found out I had no alternative except to euthanize her. No shelters would take Alta because she was so big, was a little on the old side, and had dog-aggression issues. I made close to fifty phone calls to vets, dog trainers, and friends. The final call was to an animal hospital where they walked me through the process of how she would be put to sleep.

When I hung up the phone after that painful call, with the words "injection," "paralysis," "painless," and "burial arrangements" ringing in my ears, I started praying like crazy. Seriously, like crazy. It sounds perhaps stupid to pray for a pet when I maybe should have been concentrating my prayers on more important things or situations that had a greater impact on a bigger world outside of my own tiny life. But I didn't care. I prayed and prayed and prayed. On the one hand, I prayed so hard and had more faith than not that God would somehow help me out; on the other hand, I heard the haunting echo of words someone I trusted and respected had once told me: "I don't believe God is interested in our small prayers. He's got too much on his mind to care whether you should live in a teepee in Arizona or in an igloo in Alaska or whether you should pursue a career as a doctor or a stewardess."

On day four I got a call from a sweet, young, preppy couple who adored animals and volunteered at a local shelter. They offered to help me out. (It gives me chills just thinking about it.) These folks lived in a gorgeous townhouse with—get this—a small dog and felt compassion for me in my need. They met Alta and of course immediately fell in love with her. She had that way with people. As menacing as she looked and as massive as she was, she had the sweetest personality and was undeniably likeable. No one was immune to her besetting charm. This couple, my treasured miracle, eventually took Alta under their wings. I went to visit her a year or so later, and she was still with them. She looked a little chubbier because they didn't run her as much as I used to, but she was happy. The same gargantuan bundle of joy. And she got along with the other dog marvelously.

Did God answer my prayer, or was it mere coincidence that everything worked out perfectly in the end? Would this couple have taken Alta in if I hadn't prayed? I don't know. Who knows with absolute certainty if God made something happen or if it was life or happenstance or what have you? I just remember what Paul reminded us to do: "Be thankful in all circumstances, for this is God's will for you" (1 Thess. 5:18 NLT). And I was definitely grateful.

Prayer works. It brings answers. Miracles. Before you start shaking your head and rolling your eyes, yes, I already understand that we don't always get our answers to prayers. I recognize that we will probably not get all of our miracles either. I know that stuff happens and life can be cruel and people do horrible things and life's injustices creep up in just about every corner. And I know that our prayers sometimes look and feel more like wishful thinking than anything else. But miracles happen and answers come, and nothing should stop us from believing in them.

A reality of prayer is that it can be quite discouraging when nothing seems to happen as a result. It can be gut-wrenching to devote so much time, energy, and effort in asking for stuff that doesn't come to pass. A lot of well-meaning people assert the claim that we should get all of our prayers answered as we ask. That if we have enough or the right kind of faith, we will be healed, we will get our promotions, our financial disasters will clear the next morning, and our depression will instantaneously vanish. Ouch.

Some of us don't want to hear that unanswered prayers exist, so we extinguish healthy doubt or wonder with superficial faith. Instead of offering our prayers for God to do what he will with them, we belt out praise choruses until our voices are scratchy and recite victorious Bible verses until we're blue in the face. Only through doing this, we falsely imagine, will we get our answers.

Before he was to be crucified, Jesus prayed, "Take this cup from me. Father, if there is any way out of this, please make it so" (Luke 22:42, my paraphrase). Isn't that what many of us are asking? We come to God in faith, lay our cards out on his table, and ask him to do what we want him to do. And in situations that seem bleak and hopeless, we look for loopholes to get out of them. We search for ways out of burdens. We long for quick fixes. We beg for the removal of our cup of suffering. Jesus didn't get his way out. He submitted to the Father and surrendered his will to the will of God. We must follow the same example.

I want to tell you that you will always get your answers to prayer, but I can't. I will tell you, however, that what you will definitely get is his presence. And that in itself is even greater than the greatest miracle we are looking for. I know God hears us and works through our muck for the ultimate good. Usually it doesn't look the way we would have planned it, but it's okay. Prayer is trusting that in the presence or absence of answers or miracles, we have him, and he's enough. Don't get frustrated or stop praying because life doesn't turn out the way you would have liked or think it should. Keep praying. Keep believing. Keep trusting. Don't forget we have the confidence that "we know that God causes everything to work together for the good of those who love God and are called according to his purpose for them" (Rom. 8:28 NLT).

When We're Wrong

Years ago, a friend and I used to religiously meet every Sunday at our favorite Irish pub for what we called Bloody Mary Sundays. It was a perfect way for us to regularly connect; share our thoughts on what had transpired over the past couple of days; reveal certain hidden thoughts, feelings, or secrets we needed to reveal; and assess what we needed to change, fix, or get rid of in our personal lives. Our conversations began and ended on a spiritual note. Actually, our conversations were seasoned throughout with religious overtones, and I suppose the reason is because we were (and are) both a spiritual sort of Christian.

For Christmas one year we exchanged books as gifts. I gave her one of my favorites, *Traveling Mercies* by Anne Lamott. In this book Lamott refers to herself as a "bad" Christian. Both my friend and I easily identified with that marker. There were times we thought we were bad Christians because we were both struggling with particular addictions, we considered church to be boring, and our stomachs turned at the sound of holy-roller-speak. We didn't hear the voice of God every day, we didn't always make the best decisions, and things in our lives hadn't worked out as smoothly as we assumed they would have if we were better Christians. In all fairness, though, we were both trying to improve; we really were.

I thought my friend was a pretty exceptionally bad Christian when on one particular Sunday night, she told me she didn't like God. As open, honest, accepting, and nonjudgmental as I thought I was, I was shocked by her statement. As a matter of fact, I said to myself, *How on earth could she even say that? He is so real and so loving and so alive and so great, wonderful, perfect, and so on. Surely there must be something wrong with her. I know I would never, ever say that.*

Any time I judge someone or am self-righteously appalled by someone's behavior or thought process, I find myself, with clockwork regularity, in a similar situation or mirroring the same sentiment somewhere down the road. I think God does this on purpose—to open my eyes to the flighty facets of human nature and probably to keep me humble. So two months later, I found myself not liking God very much. If it makes any sense, I loved him deep inside my heart; I just didn't like him. To me he was annoying. He didn't respond appropriately, or at all for that matter, to my constant pleas, demands, and cries. He seemed like a sinister puppet-string puller. A deity who cared more about me being and acting perfect than about the general state of my well-being. Maybe it sounds crass or unreasonable, and I'm sure on some level it is, but it was the truth of how I felt.

Why didn't I like God? I was wrong. I'd thought I heard God telling me some things in my life were going to come to fruition. In faith I believed he said that some of my prayers that have endured over the many years were going to be answered. No, a deafening, audible voice did not wake me up in the middle of the night with these brief messages; I merely felt them deep down in my spirit, as probably most of you have felt something somewhere along your spiritual journey. I was desperately seeking God with the best motives I could, and with the combination of a still, small voice in my spirit and some Bible verses I felt drawn to, I was somehow convinced of these particular things. I attributed their origin, of course, to God.

When those things didn't come to pass, I got mad. Well, frustrated is probably a better description. And hurt. Definitely hurt. Ever prayed for something and been sure you had a divine gut feeling in that situation, only to discover you were way off? Maybe the right wires got connected, just in the wrong outlets. Or the frequencies changed. Or the correct channel was on, but the connection stunk because we were in the wrong place. It's true. We can be wrong. It can happen to the best of us. Even to those who are super spiritually attuned to God.

Let me say, as I've mentioned before, that with all my heart and soul I truly believe that we can hear God speaking to us—whether through nature, through Scripture, through the inner voice, through prophetic words, through dreams, or through other sources. As Christians we're taught that eventually we learn the difference between God's words and our own words that clutter our subconscious due to our overwhelming desire to hear what we think we want to hear. As we grow and mature in faith, we better distinguish between the two.

But let's get real. None of us have a direct line to God or access to his private number or email address. He doesn't call us on the telephone from a 777 area code. He doesn't write us letters in fancy calligraphy. He doesn't give us well-written and detailed status reports of what he's thinking or feeling or has in store for us. And we, well, we all have some type of war waging within our hearts. We pray because we want something. Sometimes we want things so badly—good things and not-so-good things—that it becomes a challenge to hear exactly what God is really trying to tell us. We pray with whatever mixed motives we may have, we believe, and we think we hear God saying something to us. Sometimes we hold on to that promise with the greatest of faith and with the best of intentions. Other times, we selfishly clench it in our fists as if it has to be true, because if it's not, then we will be emotionally or otherwise destroyed and will have no choice but to think of God as a meanie or a sinister puppet-string puller.

Hearing God's voice can be a tricky task. Tricky in the sense that we, as human beings with finite minds and a wide range of shifting emotions, can equally become convinced and doubt that we hear him speaking to us. How can we say with absolute certainty what we think God, who is all knowing, all powerful, and beyond our comprehension in all ways, says? Him, who is this all-knowing, powerful, and indefinable Being. *I heard God*, we claim, and we tell our friends or our church staff or our colleagues what God said, when, and how. Is that possible? Do we really know what we hear? Can we understand supernatural dialogue? God definitely speaks to us through the Bible, and that's why it is so important to study his Word. It is probably the best resource we can use to judge what could be God's voice and what could be something entirely different. But sometimes what we hear in our spirits from him cannot be confirmed in the Bible.

There are times when we believe God is telling us, let's say, which graduate program to enroll in, who to marry, what job to take, where to live, what visions we should pursue, what purpose we should engage in, that he will heal us, that he will help us out of a legal mess, or that he will clean up an out-of-control situation that is tearing our lives apart in every which way.

When we believe God is saying a certain something, we take the proverbial leap of faith in believing whatever it is we are led to believe. My friend Josh gave me the best advice he got from his father concerning prophecies. He said, "If you want to know if a prophecy is really true or not, you have to wait to see if, in fact, it comes true." A little boring, the whole "waiting" bit, but wise and profound advice.

So if time passes and what you thought you heard from God doesn't come true—if death comes instead of healing, if the person you thought you were supposed to marry is walking down the aisle with someone else, if you didn't get that job, or if bankruptcy has been substituted for your desired financial miracle, what will you do? Get mad? Frustrated? Irritated? Depressed? Will you hate God? These are all normal and probably even expected reactions because of our humanity, but is it really fair or even wise to spend the rest of our natural lives being mad, frustrated, irritated, and depressed? Is giving up on God the best thing to do?

Here we are, these fickle, finite beings, so fervent and steadfast in our confidence that we can figure out the expectations and the actions of this super Being, this God who for the most part is unknowable. I have learned something from the times I was wrong. After my initial whining, feet-stamping, and angry attitude and being temporarily peeved at him, I realized that those things shouldn't influence my faith in him. Yeah, I was wrong. Ultimately, though, so what? Who cares? Am I going to let that dampen my love for him? Am I going to let it ruin my relationship with him? Am I going to allow that experience to define or change the core of my faith? Am I going to stop continuing to believe God for or in certain things? No. And that is what we must keep in mind when we happen to be off-base in these circumstances.

What I believe is most important is not necessarily knowing exactly what God is telling us but our belief in what we believe we are hearing. After all, the essence of Christianity is faith. Ah, faith. We believe. We take a step forward—maybe half with hesitance and half with belief, but we take that step. Our belief and possible subsequent disappointment doesn't mean God doesn't love us, or that he is not working in our lives, or that he simply does not exist. It should not hinder us from believing further. Let us not focus on being wrong or having unanswered prayers; let us rejoice in the magic that comes with simply believing. We trust. We imagine the impossible. We ask God, "Could it be true? Could it really be true?" Eyes closed and with a desperate spirit, we lunge forward. The beauty of us believing in God rests in our faith, in holding onto truth with a reckless and maybe even a crazy abandon.

Don't get discouraged when you are wrong. Keep trusting. Keep believing. Remember that there are no cookie-cutter formulas for what will result from our faith and prayers. The reality—perhaps the best reality of all—is that he is always there. Right or wrong as we are, we still must find a way to settle in his presence.

4

WHY DO I JUDGE?

How easy it is to judge rightly after one sees what evil comes from judging wrongly!

Elizabeth Gaskell

Can a blind man lead a blind man? Will they not both fall into a pit? A student is not above his teacher, but everyone who is fully trained will be like his teacher. Why do you look at the speck of sawdust in your brother's eye and pay no attention to the plank in your own eye? How can you say to your brother, "Brother, let me take the speck out of your eye," when you yourself fail to see the plank in your own eye? You hypocrite, first take the plank out of your eye, and then you will see clearly to remove the speck from your brother's eye.

Luke 6:39–42

I still dream about her. Jenny is as real today as she was when I first met her in elementary school. For a number of reasons, she was not the most attractive kid on the block. Jenny was really tall for her age and extremely skinny—skinny like she had eaten only a box of animal crackers in the last four months. Her sunken eyes and sallow skin were obvious signs of malnutrition, and most of the class used it as part of their ammunition in making fun of her.

Jenny was born with a face that was way too old for her. It was quite strange, really. Her face belonged to a teenager who had smoked, drank, and sunbathed her entire life. Jenny's gaunt face was creased with lines, like a crumpled piece of paper. She looked crinkly instead of tight. Leathery instead of supple. Weathered instead of innocent.

I remember thinking that for all of her physical defects, God could have shown some compassion and compensated her with good hair. But he didn't. Dry and frayed pieces of what looked like wire cascaded down her bony back. While my friends and I swished our luscious blonde and brunette manes around like thoroughbreds and squealed in delight showing off our cute pigtails and French braids, Jenny would slowly, almost with calculated precision, delicately twirl her frayed wires around her fingers, as if the swirling motion would help to magically transform her hair into something that could be advertised in a Pert Plus or Prell commercial.

Perhaps the most obvious flaw in her appearance, however, was something completely out of her control. Jenny had a severe form of bilateral club feet. Both of her feet were abnormally positioned in such a way that each resembled the end of a golf club. It caused her ankles to turn inward so she walked along the edges of her feet. You could tell that she concentrated intensely with every step she took, and I imagine she was in a considerable amount of pain and discomfort. It was agonizing just to watch her move. Don't think that sparked any sympathy in the classroom, though. It just sealed her "freak" status.

Jenny was the ideal target for our taunts and teases. It seemed Jenny's purpose in life was simply to entertain us with her emaciated body, old face, frizzy hair, and crooked legs. Her appearance was a welcome distraction from spelling quizzes and reading assignments. Who cared about common denominators when we could focus our attention on the girl some thought to be a weirdo who sat at the front of the room?

I admit, I did feel sorry for her. I suppose I didn't feel sorry enough, though, to defend her against the bullies. Just enough to keep quiet, to keep my amusement at bay instead of participating in the constant insults: "Here comes ugly Jenny." "There goes ugly Jenny." You could say my sign of sympathy was to ignore her for the most part. Sometimes I managed to force a half smile in her direction—but vague enough that it would be unclear whether it was meant for her or was an oh-great-it's-tater-tot-day smile. Frankly, I was concerned with what others would think if I paid attention to her, even with my fake smile.

Because I prided myself on being such a nice and friendly person, I believed I could have befriended her, or at least done a better job acknowledging her existence, if she was nicer. I was convinced the taunts would diminish to some degree if she smiled more. Or if she just acknowledged the rest of us in a more positive way instead of doing what she always did—keep her eyes at ground level, cover her face with her hair, and retreat to the sanctuary of her desk. But she didn't. She avoided our cruel gazes and kept a reasonable amount of physical distance between herself and anyone else. She especially purposefully avoided putting her deformity on display. Honestly, who could blame her?

When the final bell rang on the last day of school, we bolted out the prison doors in a race to abandon our notebooks, stubby pencils, and stupid rules. Some of us would spend time at the beach. Some would relax by turquoise pools at summer homes. Others would make meaningless crafts like Popsicle-stick houses in day camps. I'm sure every single student forgot about Jenny. I know I did.

That summer I found myself in Vacation Bible School in an Assemblies of God church two blocks away from my home. It was basically a church day camp. Though I didn't know anyone, I was quick to make friends. Once the teachers found out I played the violin, well, that just about clinched my popularity.

I remember sitting in an afternoon chapel service one particular afternoon. Only ten minutes earlier I had heard a lesson on how God is love and how we needed to follow his example. "God loves each and every one of us," the teacher pointed out. "Good or bad. Short or tall. Fat or skinny. Red, yellow, black, and white. We are all so precious in his sight." I sighed with a smug satisfaction. Even as a preteen, I felt like somewhat of a super-Christian in that moment because I knew I was a great illustration of that type of love. I was nice and kind and sweet to all. I smiled all the time. Rain or shine, you could count on my grin. This was one lesson I didn't have to take to heart.

During this service, one of the staff members made an announcement about collecting an offering for needy people. This man shared the New Testament story in Luke where Jesus is in the temple and out of nowhere something captures his eye: "As he looked up, Jesus saw the rich putting their gifts into the temple treasury" (Luke 21:1). We don't know what he's thinking as he's watching these wealthy folks drop in their hefty checks and crisp Benjamin Franklins, but his attention soon shifts to a poor widow who plunks in her alms.

Chump change, really. The echo of the two copper coins hitting the walls of the collection box is deafening. Most of us understand the moral of the story: because it was sacrificial, her denominationally small offering was considered the greatest gift of all.

Jesus doesn't focus on the wallets of the rich. He targets one type of giver—the kind that's so easy to applaud and admire on paper, yet whose example is so wretchedly difficult to live out. He says, "I tell you the truth . . . this poor widow has given more than all the rest of them. For they have given a tiny part of their surplus, but she, poor as she is, has given everything she has" (Luke 21:3–4 NLT).

After hearing the story, we kids were commissioned to walk down the aisles of the sanctuary and place our offerings at the foot of the altar. Apparently the day before, when I stayed home, all the teachers made the announcement that the next day the kids should bring with them some extra money for this special service. Not knowing this, I came empty-handed and felt somewhat stupid sitting on the pew like a bump on a log.

I watched as boy after girl catapulted out of their seats and bounced toward the front of the sanctuary. Some jingled extra change in their pockets. Some clenched a few bucks in their sweaty fists. Some even came with a Ziploc freezer bag full of pennies. And then, out of the corner of my eye, I saw something that turned my stomach inside out. For weeks I had not even noticed her, but there she was. Jenny.

Jenny hoisted herself out of her seat with a noticeable grunt. She carried the most gigantic glass jar I had ever seen in my life. It was practically half her size and full of shiny quarters, dimes, and nickels. Jenny swung one leg out of the pew and attempted to balance the weight of her scrawny frame and the gargantuan jar on that crooked mess of bone, muscle, and tissue. Just when her leg seemed like it was going to snap in half, her right leg came to the rescue and burst into the aisle in all its twisted glory.

After gaining some equilibrium, Jenny trudged down the aisle toward the altar, jar in tow. One painstaking step after another. Her mangled limbs and, perhaps much worse, her vulnerability lay naked in front of well over two hundred students and teachers. Some considered it an invitation to stare at a poor child with a deformity. As she shuffled back to her seat, I was overcome with emotion. Not only had Jenny given more money than anyone else in the entire school, but she did so knowing she would be quite the spectacle in the process.

Though as a young girl I did not quite understand the convicting power of the Holy Spirit, I believe I had one of my first God-encounters that day. I remember a picture forming in my subconscious mind. It was God beaming with pride at his beautiful child Jenny. The child, though hated and picked on by others, was loved beyond measure by the King of Kings. She was whole in his sight. She was adored by him. I remember juxtaposing that vision with my ugly behavior. How I had ignored her. How I had unabashedly exalted myself on a proverbial pedestal, basking in the glory of how great, friendly, and loving I was. How I had acted as a silent witness to the abuse she endured every single day during the school year.

I understood humility at that moment, at least as best as a child can understand. I felt so utterly small, shadowed by the reality of her generous heart and the strength of her character to be so willing to make a public offering while at the mercy of people's quick judgments about her appearance. Though this happened many years ago and I was only a little girl, I kid you not, I heard a specific question in my heart that has haunted me ever since. It is one I will never forget and one that actually prompted the writing of this chapter.

"Why did you judge her, A. J.?"

I know it may seem tough to extrapolate what judging means for a child and particularly what it meant for me at the time. It's easy, and on some level probably appropriate, to blame the foolishness and immaturity of childhood. While what I did may not have been an obvious illustration of judgmental behavior, the truth was, I had labeled her as weird, and in so doing, I deemed her unworthy of my attention, let alone friendship.

So why did I judge Jenny? I believe I judged her because I didn't know how to act around someone different from me. The concept of inner beauty was relatively foreign to me. I didn't know there was a difference between the outside shell we wear and the inner character that defines who we really are. I was fixed on the external, and because it stood in such gross contrast with what was familiar to me, it freaked me out.

Most of us made fun of other kids while growing up or were made fun of ourselves, or we may have even experienced both at different times. When we get older and become more mature, we generally don't call people horrid nicknames in public or bully others in a schoolyard sense, but we do other things that can be classified under the same category.

We define people by mistakes, by appearances, and by their weaknesses, and we refer to them by labels. Margie is the fat one. Jack is the dumb one. Ted is the alcoholic. Monica is the divorcée. We size people up before we find out what their names are. She wears too much makeup; she must be wild. He's so flirty; I bet he's cheated on his wife dozens of times. And while our assumptions may be correct once in a blue moon, categorizing people this way just means we are critical, small-minded, and judgmental. Not the greatest qualities to have.

Some of us, the minute we crawl on our bleeding hands and knees over the line into the world of recovery, forget so quickly the path that led us there. This type of amnesia also happens when we are awakened by a spiritual truth or finally "get" what our therapist has been trying to teach us for the last twenty years. Instead of soberly remembering how we got better and graciously using our gifts to help others, we start to point out their flaws, especially the subterranean ones, because we have reached what we think is an elevated sense of enlightenment. We preach in their faces about what they need to do, change, or improve, and we roll our eyes in frustration when they refuse, get offended, or are slow (in our estimation) in getting better. Never mind that we were in the same boat not quite five minutes earlier.

Others of us have a knack for forgetting the reality of our fragile, sinful nature. We are so seemingly perfect, we pretend we don't have any weaknesses, and so everyone else's are ours for the attacking. "She is so undisciplined." "Why does he have to talk so much?" "What? She drank three glasses of wine?" "He should just put down the slice of pizza!" C'mon. Don't we all bear claim to a foible or two or ten? Don't we all need the grace of God as much as our neighbor? Don't we all make stupid mistakes or fall prey to some temptation?

The rest of us have a knack for pointing out the failings in others, at supersonic speed, while our own skeletons rattle violently in our closets. Or, as Jesus so eloquently put it, while a plank rests quite visibly in our own eye.

A Time for Trusted Wounds

Make no mistake: judging, in an appropriate sense, is necessary in certain situations. There is good judging and bad judging. Bad judging results from moral superiority, when we label the worth of others by things that don't create their true identity, when we snub our noses at someone for their failures, when we pick at their weaknesses when we've got a two-by-four sticking out of our eye. Yet we must be careful that we do not turn a blind eye toward a loved one who is engaging in behavior that is clearly self-destructive or immoral. If you have a friend who is destroying her life with drugs or alcohol, for instance, you would be a terrible confidant not to address the issue. But you would be a hypocrite if you shook your finger in her face and told her, "Stop. Just say no to drugs," after you have just smoked a joint together.

In my late teens I had a best friend. We shared a very codependent relationship. She had a boyfriend who wasn't around much, and because I was, we became each other's partner in crime. While I'm sure our relationship had some healthy aspects, we were very needy. And not necessarily needy for each other. We ached to feed our addictions and have a companion by our side who would understand, not make us stop. So we drank. A lot.

When I found out she puked her food on occasion, by golly, I had just found me a friend for life. We would drink, eat ourselves silly, visit the porcelain god, and then do it all over again. I remember one time when the toilet at her apartment was slow, so we had to be strategic on how to get rid of our food. We decided to throw up in plastic bags. She and I were women who loved fancy clothes and expensive things, and here we were, a pair of well-put-together blondes barfing our pizza and vodka into a Hefty bag, careful not to let random chunks of vomit splatter and ruin our three-hundred-dollar shoes. It was quite a sight.

We were both very bitter young ladies. We hated men for using us. We hated our church for judging us. We hated society for telling us we were too chubby. And, of course, we hated ourselves.

We constantly made jokes about how we were going to end up at the Betty Ford clinic. We laughed about suicide. We imagined going out in a blaze of glory. In hindsight, our behavior was beyond destructive even in light of our share of good, sober, and abstinent moments.

The relationship dissolved in time when I moved to another state. Neither of us broke out of the relationship because we wanted to focus on our health or emotional well-being. But realistically speaking, that was probably the only way either of us could have gotten better at the time. Could she have told me to stop drinking? Could I have told her to stop throwing up? Can the blind lead the blind?

But what if you are in a situation where someone's destructive behavior is negatively influencing your own life and, if you continue the relationship, there is a good chance of you becoming an enabler or codependent? What do you do? Simple: you must separate yourself from the situation. There is usually no other choice. You've gotta cut the cord. I'm not a psychologist or a pastor, so I'm not going to even attempt to list some guidelines to piggyback common sense. You can talk to those professionals about discovering what the fine line is between being Christlike and cutting someone loose to trash their own lives in your absence.

Let me talk about calling someone out in love instead of judging someone when you have pretty rotten motives. Proverbs 27:6 says, "Wounds from a friend can be trusted, but an enemy multiplies kisses." Good friends are truth-seekers. They are tough on you when appropriate. They help bring to light dark realities. They are not afraid—or at least are more willing than afraid—to recognize and challenge harmful or unhealthy patterns in your life. As a matter of fact, I would be willing to say that if we truly value our intimate friendships, we would actually want and ask for our friends to appropriately strip away the wool we've pulled over our own eyes.

My sister Vivien and I share a very special relationship. We are very lucky sisters who actually get along, like each other, and enjoy spending time with one another. We have been best friends for a good sixteen years and have had only one major fight. We didn't speak to each other for over a week, and, ironically, neither of us can now remember what caused the argument. (This is usually the case for most of us, isn't it?)

Vivien and I lived together for many years until I moved to New Jersey and her life took an exotic twist and she took off to Thailand. While on opposite sides of the globe, we still manage to communicate with each other at least four days out of the week. Our conversations last a minimum of thirty minutes. Somehow, over all the years and through our unique life journeys, we still have not run out of things to say.

Every so often I'll get a special phone call from her. It's the "I need you to be tough on me" kind. She'll share something that she is struggling with (morally or otherwise), ask for my thoughts, and welcome my tough-love approach. I will always tell her the truth, even if it hurts. There has never been a time when she has refused my opinions or guidance. I think this is because she knows that I love her unconditionally, that I have supported her through thick and thin, that I have always been her advocate, and that I still believe in her.

In turn, I give Vivien confessional phone calls. Because I am somewhat of a private person, I will usually keep what some would call the juicy tidbits about my life to myself. What they are, really, are areas that show my vulnerability. Things I do that are bad for me, things I am a step away from doing that are bad for me, thought patterns that have the power to destroy my sanity, even feelings that scare the living daylights out of me. All honest, raw, and real stuff that, quite frankly, most of us would have difficulty in sharing with anyone.

I want to live a healthy life and have a meaningful and purposeful future, so I confess these things to her because I know she will set me straight. This time Vivien will tell *me* the truth, and I know it's always in love. She may tell me things I don't want to hear, or yell at me for doing something stupid, or warn me to run away from a particular temptation, but it's okay. It's still the truth, I need to hear it, and it's wisely embraced because it's coming from a confidant who thinks the world of me.

We all need to have and be that type of person. We especially all need to have the kind of attitude that makes us willing to say things to our close friends like, "I need you to help me. I need you to be tough on me. I need you to tell me what I'm doing wrong. I need you to look into my eyes and tell me I need to back away from this situation. I need you to take the speck out of my eye."

In Ephesians Paul writes, "Speaking the truth in love, we will in all things grow up into . . . Christ" (4:15). We can't grow up in our faith without confessing truth. This means having the purest of motives, and let's be honest, none of us have or are going to have the purest of motives all of the time. The psalmist cried out, "Search me, O God, and know my heart" (Ps. 139:23). This is something we need to do regularly. We need to be searchable followers of Christ, willing to allow him to penetrate right to our core to see if our hearts are in the right place.

Sometimes less obvious signs of judging appear in ways that we may never recognize unless we are paying close attention to what is going on inside of ourselves. For example, while we may be saying something to someone that may be ultimately helpful to them, are we truly doing it with the right intentions? Are we speaking the truth in love? Do we genuinely care about their healthiness? Do we really love them enough to want to help them? Or do we secretly find pleasure in seeing their flaws and pretend to be sincere in our admonishment? Is it possible that we just might want to stick it to them a little?

It would do us all a lot of good to be so open to the Spirit that we ask him to search us and know our hearts. It may be the only way we will be able to feel God tapping us on our shoulders and saying, "I know you're trying to say the right thing to warn your friend, but it is being fueled by wrong motives. So why are you really judging?"

The Green-Eyed Monster

A few years ago I got a phone call from an old and dear friend I hadn't spoken to in a while. I always admired her for her keen ability to quickly slice through people's superficial exteriors, their glib chit-chat, and the defensive walls they put up. She doesn't have time for nonsense and always gets straight to the point. That being said, her sense of directness influences her own persona as she is unable to tiptoe or talk her way around what she struggles with or obsesses about. It's really a great quality to have.

So when she called me, after a minute or two of the affectionate volley of "how *are* you's?" she launched into what was really on her mind. "I'm in love. He has a girlfriend that he's living with and they just had a baby. But I'm in love and I have no intention of breaking it off with him."

Because I had always appreciated her candor and I loved her like a sister, my initial reaction wasn't anywhere near, "You dumb little tramp. How on earth did you let yourself get into this mess?" I let her talk about it because I knew she had no one else to talk about it with since this man was pretty well-known in the community they lived in. I was also sure to voice my disapproval, as this was a relationship that was likely unable to produce any sort of good. It was a dead-end road. I did what a good and true friend would do. I told her to run away from him, in every sense of the word, as fast as her feet could carry her.

A year and a half later, after I had painfully stomached a handful of letdowns in basically stupid relationships and had been sucker punched by the love of my life, my friend called me again. I'll be honest: a part of me—a pretty big part—was happy to hear from her because I believed she was drinking the same cup of pain, tears, and bitterness as I was. Surely the affair she was involved in a year and a half ago could not have lasted beyond two seconds, or at most a few weekends of hot and steamy sex.

We entered into another round of "how are you's," and this time I vocally purged my emotional distress in her ears. Hollywood romances didn't exist. Prince Charmings were truly fictional. Love was stupid. Men were idiots. In a blow to my gut, she didn't return the favor. Instead, my friend shared how she was still in love. How she had never met a man like this in her life. How he was leaving the live-in girlfriend. How they were going to move in together. Yada yada yada. And that was when, in a deep, dark, and highly sensitive crevasse in my heart, I started to judge in an incredibly ugly fashion.

What an idiot. Doesn't she know he's just using her for sex? Inside I fumed and raged and raged and fumed. I was infuriated with God for letting her have butterflies in her tummy when I had knots in mine. How dare he send her romance when my rose garden was a dry, pathetic nest of thorns and bugs? How come she got the blessing of love and I was still alone after all these years? It was unfair!

I didn't share the expanse of my thoughts with her, of course. I continued to give her sound and stable advice to pack up her bags and defect from the relationship while I wallowed in my jealousy. Although no one was privy to my judging thoughts except me, I knew they were there. They haunted me. They pitched tents, camped out, and ordered take-out. They began to nibble at my insides until I realized the full-fledged air of judgment I had toward my friend.

I was saying the same things I had offered in our first conversation. I sincerely related how you could fall in love with someone who could be really wrong for you and find yourself, on purpose or otherwise, crippled in a bad situation. I also shared how her relationship was simply too messy and she had the responsibility, for her own sanity, to get out, even though it was hard and perhaps even on some level unfair. But awful things were buried beneath my words. I found myself irritated with her. While my words were suggesting one thing, my attitude was saying entirely something else. It was obvious I was snubbing my nose at her.

Why did I judge? Because I was disappointed with God. Because I thought I deserved what she had. Because I was tired of being alone. Because I was jealous. Ever judge someone out of jealousy? Deep down inside you want something they have, and because you feel they have not appropriately gotten it or are not properly stewarding or appreciating it, you feel justified in crucifying their actions. You may not nail their body to a tree, but you regard them in an unfavorable light.

I was judging my friend, who was in a very terrible mess, not wholly out of love or concern for her well-being. I was simply bothered by the fact that I didn't have what she had. Yes, even if what she had may not have been all that great. The green-eyed monster will tell you the grass is always greener on the other side.

Why do I judge? Why do you judge? What great questions to ask to find out what we really think and believe and to expose our own struggles, doubts, anxieties, and anger.

You Make Me Look Good

One time I had lunch with some good friends of mine. I had grown up with them, and we had recently reconnected after some-odd years. They were fun, they were neat, and I always had such a great time with them. During our lunch we laughed, joked around, and ate a fantastic meal, and most of us drank cosmopolitans. And sangria. And more cosmopolitans. And some red wine. And more cosmopolitans. I believe that right before I started having memory loss from the exorbitant amount of alcohol I was consuming, a handful of us downed a few shots of some kind of liquor that smelled like urine and tasted like gasoline.

Before I continue, let me say that none of us were drinkers. I'm not making excuses or trying to justify our excessive drinking, but none of us were alcoholics by any stretch. We were responsible citizens of the community. We were probably all just a little stressed out in the different areas of our lives, and we enjoyed a much-needed respite from reality in the company of good friends.

Yes, in that process, our self-control definitely took a leave of absence. At some point—which is never a very good point—we found ourselves devoid of even the tiniest amount of reason and restraint. So we kept drinking. When I was still somewhat sober, I noticed something interesting that we each did at different times. Whenever one of us noticed our glass was nearing empty, we hesitantly looked around to see if anybody else was ordering something. Soon enough, someone in the group would summon the waiter and ask, "Can I get another one?" Then the rest of us would breathe a sigh of relief and exclaim, "Yeah, one more for me too." As long as everyone else was drinking, it was okay, especially okay for me. It made perfect sense and made me feel more comfortable about being a tad out of control.

I remember the waiter dropping off the check at the table, and that's pretty much it. The rest of the evening was a blur that left behind random snippets of memory. For those of us who were pretty smashed, the events of the night were retold to us in pretty humiliating details. I, needless to say, was utterly mortified. Watching a completely inebriated woman trying to communicate intelligent thoughts while words disappear in slurred speech and the absence of lucidity is not a pretty picture. My mom always told me that a drunk lady is not a classy lady. My mom's a very wise woman.

If what one of my friends said is true, I threw up in a kitchen sink and admitted a secret crush I had on someone. And I babbled on incessantly for hours about nothing. I was a blubbery, sloppy fool.

So back to the drinking. Yes, I realize it could have been worse, but here's my point. When I talked with one of the ladies the next morning, we both failed miserably in trying to recapture some of the blank spaces in our memory. She did, however, relay stories that were told to her by her sober husband. That's how I knew I threw up in a kitchen sink. Honestly, it would have been better not to know. I've always hated that wretched knot in your stomach you feel after doing something incredibly stupid . . . something that everyone sees.

In the process of pathetically trying to make ourselves feel better by neutralizing the situation in different ways, we said things like, "Well, we weren't *that* bad. I mean, at least we were with good friends. So what? We're all adults and responsible. So we drank too much? Big deal!" But our conversation quickly took a different bend. We started to compare ourselves with the other people involved by judging them more harshly than we judged ourselves. "Well, she was passed out before we were." "He drank like a fish in front of the baby." "That one started out with vodka." I was fully aware of what we were doing, which was making ourselves look good by making others look bad, yet I continued to contribute to the conversation. A part of me couldn't help it. Horrible and wrong as it was, it was definitely making me feel better.

Why do I judge? Because judging someone else's actions more severely than mine makes me look good. It takes the sting away from questioning my character. It releases me from a thorough internal self-examination. It keeps me away from doing the painful work. It removes some of that aching in my conscience. Sure, it makes me a hypocrite, but it also prevents me from having to make peace with the reflection in the mirror.

Why do you judge? Are you scared of your failures? Are you frustrated with your own self? Are you lonely? These are all hard questions to have to muck through to find answers. But doing so makes us better people. It makes us grow in Christ. It exposes the truth of our lives so the truth of God can better shine through.

Our faith is messy enough with its own twists, turns, ups, and downs without needing to bully our way into the life of the gal down the street who may or may not be living with her boyfriend. Pay attention to what you say. More importantly, pay attention to what is going on inside your heart. When you find yourself saying or thinking things that are less than pleasant or edifying, ask yourself, "Why do I judge?" You'll be surprised what you'll find.

Jesus, as always, gave the best advice: "You must be compassionate, just as your Father is compassionate. Do not judge others, and you will not be judged. Do not condemn others, or it will all come back against you. Forgive others, and you will be forgiven. Give, and you will receive. Your gift will return to you in full—pressed down, shaken together to make room for more, running over, and poured into your lap. The amount you give will determine the amount you get back" (Luke 6:36–38 NLT).

5

THE GIFT OF THE BROKEN

Our Lord, you break the bows of warriors, but you give strength
to everyone who stumbles.

1 Samuel 2:4 CEV

I have a problem with shallow "super-Christians." I'm sure you
know the type very well. They always have great posture and flaw-
less hairstyles. They wear trendy ties and bleach their teeth. Okay,
maybe I'm being unfair in those descriptions, but they definitely do
have a transparent spiritual answer for every nonspiritual question.
They are extraordinarily nice to you in a patronizing sort of way,
and their language is always syrupy. They pray for your problems
in one breath and in the next feel sorry—the poor-pathetic-you
kind of sorry—for not getting it right. The worst thing they ever
did was probably lie about their weight or their age. Life has been
pretty steady—not perfect or trouble-free by any means, just void

of the kind of life experiences that can serve to threaten a Pollyan-naish existence.

Then there are the rest of us—the ones who are very aware that the treasures of Christ are carried within "jars of clay" (2 Cor. 4:7). They're not necessarily the prettiest of containers and look shabby and out-of-place next to a Tiffany glass vase or even a cachepot from Pottery Barn. But who or what are we anyway? Perfect? Near perfect? Seemingly perfect? No. We are all human beings who are born with weaknesses and splattered with flaws and messy experiences as we continue to blow out our birthday candles. Through our odysseys in valleys and mountains and in sunlight and shadows, most of us acquire cracks on our superficial surface. What are most of us? Simple: we are broken.

When I think about brokenness, I don't think about it as having no self-esteem or pooh-poohing our humanness. I certainly don't believe we need to weep and wail over our failings and sit on Main Street wearing a burlap sack and tearing our hair out by the roots. I don't think we need to return compliments by saying, "Oh no, I am just a wretch, a miserable worm. A poor excuse for a person." I'm talking about being aware of our brokenness in the context of being aware who works in and through us. The Bible tells us Christ's strength is made perfect in our weakness (see 2 Cor. 12:9). Do we really get it, though? For some of us, it is painful or embarrassing to admit our shortcomings and struggles. We try so hard to be perfect, look good, color in the lines at all times, and hide our vulnerabilities under lock and key so no sign of possible frailty is ever exposed. What Achilles' heel? Oh, that bandage? Oh, please. That's the new trend this winter!

I suppose we don't need to advertise our life cracks on our sleeves or slap patches on our skin that illustrate the hard roads we've traveled. But we also don't need to pretend we are faith-based superheroes who only need Christ every once in a blue moon because we are naturally wise, self-controlled, disciplined, and without addictive tendencies. Because we can live blameless lives practically effortlessly. On our own. Thanks, Jesus, for your grace and strength and all. But I'll only need it every six months; otherwise, I'm pretty capable myself. Thanks but no thanks.

The book of Genesis shares with us the story of Jacob. Jacob is born "with his hand grasping [his twin brother] Esau's heel" (Gen. 25:26). His mother appropriately names him Jacob, which means "heel grabber," and he does a pretty good job of living up to his name as he grows up. Jacob is always grabbing onto things that aren't his and quickly gains a reputation for being a swindler, a cheat, a shyster. He creatively cons his twin brother out of the birthright that is rightfully his and then proceeds to deceitfully take away the blessing of their father, Isaac. As a result, a double-crossed and fuming Esau vows to kill Jacob, who begins a literal flight for his life.

Through a series of events, Jacob flees his homeland and ends up working with a guy named Laban. It is a colorful narrative of what comes around goes around as Laban is quite the cheat himself. He gives Jacob a run for his money in the art of double-dealing. Among other things, Laban tricks Jacob into marrying the wrong daughter, and Jacob pays dearly for the scam by working his butt off for the guy for seven more years.

As time goes by, Jacob eventually sires a pretty large family and heads a successful business raising flocks of sheep and other livestock. He is a self-made go-getter, an entrepreneurial success story. But deep down inside, he is itching for home. Though Jacob is reaping the lucrative benefits of his innate skills and abilities and his hard work, the image of Esau is still very much alive in his mind. He wants to go back to his roots, find his brother, and make some long-overdue peace. I would guess that although about twenty years has passed, not even that length of time could erase the pain and embarrassment that had festered under Esau's skin. It's time for Jacob to face the music.

To make a long story short, Jacob makes the trek back to his homeland in a motorcade of his familial entourage and acquired wealth. But truth be told, the guy is shaking in his boots. Jacob sends two messengers ahead of him carrying fancy gifts for Esau to try to proactively smooth things over. Maybe a Rolex watch or a shiny Maserati would help in erasing part of the ugly past. When the men come back with their report, they simply tell Jacob, "We went to your brother Esau, and now he is coming to meet you, and four hundred men are with him" (Gen. 32:6). Four hundred men?

Jacob gulps, feels his insides knot with fear, and erupts in a full-fledged freak-out. He immediately goes into strategy mode and devises a plan to, plainly, save his skin and that of at least half of the family and workers who accompanied him. "In great fear and distress Jacob divided the people who were with him into two groups, and the flocks and herds and camels as well. He thought, 'If Esau comes and attacks one group, the group that is left may escape'" (Gen. 32:7–8). What he does next is what we all do when we find ourselves in a pickle absent of options, escape routes, and even a flicker of hope. Jacob collapses to his knees and cries out in a desperate prayer. Among other things, he pleads with God to remember the covenant God had made with him some time ago. He begs for help. He appeals for deliverance. He admits his unworthiness.

That night he sends the two groups ahead toward what he hoped was safety and finds himself in solitude. This is where I think the story gets interesting. It is strangely chronicled in a relatively matter-of-fact manner, without much pomp and circumstance:

> So Jacob was left alone, and a man wrestled with him till daybreak. When the man saw that he could not overpower him, he touched the socket of Jacob's hip so that his hip was wrenched as he wrestled with the man. Then the man said, "Let me go, for it is daybreak."
> But Jacob replied, "I will not let you go unless you bless me."
> The man asked him, "What is your name?"
> "Jacob," he answered.
> Then the man said, "Your name will no longer be Jacob, but Israel, because you have struggled with God and with men and have overcome."
> Jacob said, "Please tell me your name."
> But he replied, "Why do you ask my name?" Then he blessed him there.
> So Jacob called the place Peniel, saying, "It is because I saw God face to face, and yet my life was spared."
> The sun rose above him as he passed Peniel, and he was limping because of his hip.
>
> Genesis 32:24–31

This story is rich with depth, and many have gleaned from it a variety of great lessons and truths. So who was Jacob's wrestling partner? A human being? An angel? Jacob's alter ego? I believe it was God. It seems pretty clear that he purposely put Jacob's hip out of socket and made him walk with a limp that ailed him the rest of his life. At least that is what I infer from a verse in Hebrews that says, "It was by faith that Jacob, when he was old and dying, blessed each of Joseph's sons and bowed in worship *as he leaned on his staff*" (Heb.11:21 NLT, emphasis added).

I believe the heel-grabbing swindler knew this to be a divine wrestling match, and so he wrestled like a superior athlete with all of his might. God is not a phantom to Jacob, nor a storybook character, nor a flimsy cloud on top of a mountain; he is a challenger. I can picture him gently lifting Jacob's chin up with his finger and firmly saying, "You want a fight, my boy? How bad do you want me?" And Jacob wants God bad enough to grab hold of him with his sturdy grip and fierce attitude. Something we ought to be regularly reminded of in our own lives.

So they wrestle—grunting, grappling, and sprawling—and God, recognizing Jacob as a natural fighter with some serious don't-mess-with-me ability, knows what he has to do to put Jacob where he belongs. Jacob must be broken. Not in a pathetic way to rob him of self-esteem. Not in a mean way to punish his wrongs. But in a way that would prompt Jacob to realize how seriously he was in need of God and how his strengths were no match for God. So God puts Jacob's hip out of joint. And Jacob does what God had hoped (and knew) he would do. He stops grappling and fighting and starts clinging in utter desperation. Jacob is not fighting anymore; he is holding on for dear life.

Finally God says, "Let me go." Was this a challenge, perhaps? A test of sorts to see whether Jacob would timidly throw his hands up in surrender or grip the flesh of his heavenly Father even tighter? "I will not let you go," a tormented Jacob cries as he sucks in sharp, painful breaths and his stance weakens from his broken hip and debilitating muscle cramps. "Not until you bless me."

Jacob is stripped at that moment of everything that had created and multiplied his confidence. I believe he needed, in his own particular way, to fight for what he wanted, which was the manifestation and blessing of his Maker, with genuine sweat, blood, and tears—the hunger of true desperation. A blessed man when he crawls away from the mat, Jacob takes with him a souvenir. It's not a T-shirt that says, "I wrestled with God at Peniel and survived." Jacob is maimed. He has a limp that is impossible for him not to feel and for others not to notice. He is broken. Broken, but a living illustration that he is better off leaning on a staff for the rest of his life knowing God is on his side than standing on his own merit. Each wobbly step he took, Jacob knew God was with him. His brokenness had to have preceded the blessing. God wouldn't have had it any other way.

If you live life long enough, you'll endure at least one traumatic experience that leaves you somewhat broken. Perhaps the death of a loved one. A debilitating disease. Parental abandonment. An addiction that is another word for slow suicide. A two-hour mistake that cost you a lifetime of consequences. You may also be blindsided and fall into temptation, have difficulty emulating Jesus's perfect character, or struggle with depression. As a Christian, especially, you may come face-to-face with a mediocre or weakening faith. Prayers seem useless. Scriptures once used to empower and encourage are seemingly rendered ineffective or even confusing. God's presence, which was once as real as the touch of your own flesh, will seem to have wandered into oblivion. Doubt comes waltzing into the mind, maybe as little as faint drops of rain or as powerful as a hurricane.

Cracks the size of baby eyelashes appear on our fragile clay pots. Some start getting longer. The loveliness of our exterior diminishes into something drab and dull, and for whatever reason, we become broken. The strength of our self-made spirituality, our self-controlled behavior, and the talents that we may have relied upon has vanished. Perhaps we even want to give up on life, on God, on ourselves. Broken people sometimes have a hard time finding a comfortable resting place in a church. It's no wonder the

Bible defines the church as the body of Christ, not a magnificently built four-walled structure filled with seemingly perfect people. It's no wonder, reading through the Gospels, that the forlorn, the lonely, the weary, and the almost-faithless people found Jesus so approachable.

Why? He didn't pay attention to their Dolce & Gabbana sandals or their impressive résumé. Neither, of course, did he notice the dirt in their nails or their stuttering speech. Christ met people in the strangest places, in the deepest parts of who they were. In these deepest parts, however messed up, struggling, hurting, failing, or doubting, is where the truth of who we are lies. And sure, it's usually not a sight for sore eyes.

Our hearts, our honesty, our true selves is what Jesus deems our Sunday best. I am impressed with churches, pastors, faith leaders, and regular Christian folk who are antiseptic examples of living victorious and almost perfect lives. However, their presence doesn't mean the absence of Christians who have a tough time with their faith and with their lives. When God seems so far away, as a result of whatever it is we are going through, it doesn't mean he has left us. It doesn't mean that we are unworthy, or that we have lost our Christian faith, or that we are "bad" Christians. The broken shouldn't feel left behind, although that is most often the case. I don't want them to be ignored or slighted. Broken Christians exist. I know; I've got my own battle scars.

I like what Paul has to say about being carriers of the Spirit of God. In 2 Corinthians 4 he writes, "We now have this light shining in our hearts, but we ourselves are like fragile clay jars containing this great treasure. This makes it clear that our great power is from God, not from ourselves. We are pressed on every side by troubles, but we are not crushed. We are perplexed, but not driven to despair. We are hunted down, but never abandoned by God. We get knocked down, but we are not destroyed. Through suffering, our bodies continue to share in the death of Jesus so that the life of Jesus may also be seen in our bodies" (vv. 7–10 NLT). Our sufferings are as individual and as unique as we are. We are fortunate enough to be able to be in relationship with One whose purpose on earth was to suffer so he could understand our brokenness.

The Road to Emmaus

"He took some bread and gave thanks to God for it. Then he broke it in pieces and gave it to the disciples, saying, 'This is my body, which is given for you. Do this to remember me'" (Luke 22:19 NLT). At the Last Supper, Jesus symbolizes the redemption of humanity by the breaking of bread and drinking of wine. Remember me, he says, always remember me. With crumbs of bread splattering the supper table, he foreshadows not just his torn flesh but something much worse—his heartbreak.

Later that night, only hours before he would be arrested, Jesus goes with a handful of his disciples to a place called the Mount of Olives to pray, something he did quite frequently. It is clear that this is no ordinary prayer time. Matthew tells us that Jesus is "sorrowful and troubled" (26:37). Burdened by the next scene in the final act of his earthly life, the crucifixion, Jesus wretchedly presses his followers, "My soul is overwhelmed with sorrow to the point of death. Stay here and keep watch with me" (Matt. 26:38). His disciples, unfortunately, fail the task miserably and fall asleep. Before you start to judge them and call them total morons for snoozing at such a critical juncture of time, you must realize they weren't just taking a nap. They weren't bored out of their minds or disloyal to Jesus's request for their companionship. Matthew writes they were sleeping "because their eyes were heavy" (26:43). Luke tells us, more graphically, that they were "exhausted from grief" (Luke 22:45 NLT). Maybe you would have stayed awake, maybe not. Just give these guys a break.

So here Jesus is. I'm sure he can already feel the unbearable weight of a cross that will soon be tied to his raw, bruised, and bleeding shoulders. And I'm sure his ears are haunted by the faint echoes of the hammer that will soon drive nails into his wrists and feet. Jesus is fiercely struggling in the midst of an eternal battle, human flesh and divinity at war—the flesh he chose to take on and the God that he was. With a hoarse voice and a sorrowful heart, Jesus cries to his Father, " 'If you are willing, please take this cup of suffering away from me. Yet I want your will to be done, not mine.' Then an angel from heaven appeared and strengthened him. He prayed more fervently, and he was in such agony of spirit that his sweat fell to the ground like great drops of blood" (Luke 22:42–44 NLT).

I believe this is where we really see the beginning of his brokenness. The truth of the redemption plan is sinking in, and it's nowhere near a walk in the park. Soon enough, at the peak of the crucifixion experience, Jesus would be painfully vocal in expressing a sense of abandonment from God when he would cry out, "Eloi, Eloi, lama sabachthani?" or "My God, my God, why have You forsaken me?" (Matt. 27:46). This is utter heartbreak.

Luke narrates something that happened after the resurrection that makes me think about the brokenness of Christ. Two men, who were actually followers of Jesus, are walking to a village called Emmaus. Luke writes that sadness was written across their faces. As the visibly perturbed pair is walking, they share a conversation about their dead Messiah—the one who was supposed to be their cure-all, their hope, their religious warrior, their answer.

They remain glum when a stranger, who unbeknownst to them is Jesus, joins them on their journey. Aware of their troubled spirits, he asks them what's wrong, and they spout off a depressing monologue. "You must be the only person in Jerusalem who hasn't heard about all the things that have happened there the last few days . . . to Jesus, the man from Nazareth. . . . He was a prophet who did powerful miracles, and he was a mighty teacher in the eyes of God and all the people. But our leading priests and other religious leaders handed him over to be condemned to death, and they crucified him. We had hoped he was the Messiah who had come to rescue Israel" (Luke 24:19–21 NLT).

Jesus listens to them and says, among other things, "Didn't Christ have to die and suffer? Wasn't it supposed to be part of the plan?" (see Luke 24:25). Imagine that, a Savior who suffers. A God who loves us so much that he is willing to clothe himself with humanity—with abandonment, with hurt, with brokenness, with the same types of emotions you and I experience.

Jesus pretends he plans to go farther on his trip when these two men ask him to stay with them, to rest a while, and to spend the night at their house. Luke states that they practically begged him to stay (see Luke 24:9). Some moments later, after Jesus agrees to hang out a while, all three of them are seated at a dinner table, and as the custom goes, they break bread. At this moment they recognize him. "When he was at the table with them, he took bread, gave thanks, broke it and began to give it to them. Then their eyes were opened and they recognized him, and he disappeared from their sight" (Luke 24:30–31).

With the breaking of bread, the brokenness of body and spirit, they knew Christ. They figured out who he was. They remembered him. The Bible states that before they officially knew who Jesus was, their hearts were mysteriously touched by his presence (see Luke 24:32). This is the same type of gnawing of heart we experience when encountering Christ. Something different. Special. Holy. Loving. Pure. No strings attached. Just as doubting Thomas knew Jesus by placing his fingers in Christ's side and hands, these two men knew him completely through the breaking of bread, of flesh and bone, and of spirit. And then he disappeared, the Bible says, but remained ever-present in Spirit.

Finding Jesus at His Feet

Folks who are afflicted with addictions, particularly those involved in twelve-step programs, know full well the experience of brokenness. While people normally attribute sex, alcohol, food, and drug addictions to a sort of temporary recreational satisfaction of unnecessary and harmful compulsions, the indulgence is more anesthetic than anything. Some find their pains, fears, and experiences too fragile to address, let alone deal with in a rational and therapeutic manner. And so the only reasonable solution is to medicate, with whatever and anything. Medicate with cocaine, medicate with cartons of non-filter Camels, or in my specific case, medicate with a little bit of sex, a little bit of alcohol, and a harrowing monster of bulimia.

When God seemed as distant and imperceptible to me as green Martians swing dancing on Jupiter, some parts of my spiritual faith and persona started to crumble, and others started to become overly sensitive. I was continually hurt, angry, and broken from God's seeming absence and inability to remove my addictions with the snap of his holy fingers. You would think that the further I fell into this addictive pit, the further I would push away this silent Savior. On the contrary, I pulled this Unknown as close to me as I could. It was a desperate trust, a reckless holding on to something so hard that my knuckles turned white. Or maybe he was holding on to me, for whatever strange reason.

I remember one evening when I visited my favorite pub and had one too many shots of liquor, then walked to my car in the wee hours of the morning and passed a Spanish evangelical church. It wasn't the church that caught my eye; it was the steps. I sat down on the steps and began to cry. If the church had been open, I probably wouldn't have gone inside but would have remained glued to the rows of concrete.

Even in the midst of my drunken stupor, I could not have numbed myself enough to ignore a pressing thought about the beyond-measure love of God. It wasn't a passing thought, the type that leaves your mind as quickly as it enters it, but something deeper, almost to the point of being overbearing. The lyrics from the hymn "The Love of God" abruptly came to mind:

> The love of God is greater far
> Than tongue or pen can ever tell.
> It goes beyond the highest star
> And reaches to the lowest hell.
> The guilty pair, bowed down with care,
> God gave His Son to win.
> His erring child He reconciled
> And pardoned from his sin.
>
> Could we with ink the ocean fill,
> And were the skies of parchment made,
> Were every stalk on earth a quill,
> And every man a scribe by trade,

To write the love of God above
Would drain the ocean dry.
Nor could the scroll contain the whole
Though stretched from sky to sky.

O love of God, how rich and pure!
How measureless and strong!
It shall forevermore endure
The saints' and angels' song.[1]

All of a sudden the church steps turned from cold, gray slabs of concrete into the feet of Christ. And I wanted to sit on the steps and feel as near to Jesus, at his feet, as I could. The same feet that trod hundreds of miles to heal the sick, redeem the lost, and mend the broken. The same feet that were once kissed, anointed, and wept over by a broken, hurting woman who had burst through the doors during a dinner party where Jesus was the guest of honor.

She had probably overheard—through public though secretive whispers—that he was going to be in that place at that moment and figured it was her only chance. For what? A rendezvous with a renowned spiritual leader? An encounter with a mystic or magician? Or an opportunity to offer her broken self, her true being, to the One who accepts and redeems such things?

The host of this party—a Pharisee, according to Luke—silently questions this woman's intrusive entrance. The woman ignores him and proceeds to wash Jesus's feet with a perfumed oil that cost her an unimaginable amount of wages. It was all she knew to give him. It was all she had to give him. While she continues to weep and wash his feet with her greasy ointment, her tears, and her brokenness, the overzealous host mentally hisses, "If this man [Jesus] were a prophet, he would know who is touching him and what kind of woman she is—that she is a sinner" (Luke 7:39). The "sinner" continues to weep and wash, as if she was supposed to stop. She is called a sinner, as if no one else, including this accusatory man, ever wore such a label.

She starts anointing Jesus from the bottom up—from the bottom of her pain, her emptiness, and her unbearable longing for forgiveness, joy, and love. She kisses him from the bottom of his feet, and Jesus is immensely touched. He gently reproves the host, "Do you see this woman? I came into your house. You did not give me any water for my feet, but she wet my feet with her tears and wiped them with her hair. You did not give me a kiss, but this woman, from the time I entered, has not stopped kissing my feet. You did not put oil on my head, but she has poured perfume on my feet. Therefore, I tell you, her many sins have been forgiven—for she loved much. But he who has been forgiven little loves little" (Luke 7:44–47).

Please do not misunderstand me. I am not offering proverbial kudos to the sinner in all of us. I am not saying that you can experience the fullness of grace and redemption only after being as sinful as possible. I am simply speaking to the people who have already found themselves broken for reasons only they know. The men and women who don't like where they are but are there because it's easier than being anywhere else. Being broken reveals a severe longing, a desperate need that can only be resolved through Christ, from the bottom of the pit up. This woman was the sinner in all of us—the liar, the addict, the promiscuous, the legalistic, the judgmental, the unkind, the selfish. She found her saving grace at his feet in the same way I found my heart melting at the thought of his measureless love on those random church steps.

Many anonymous souls can only come as near to the church as the church steps. As near to religion as his feet. Our brokenness, when met with the longing that is really a longing for God, creates a rendezvous in the strangest places and at the strangest times. The beauty is that he meets us where we are. This woman who barged into a dinner party uninvited did so with humility, with repentance, and with reckless abandon. She needed Christ in the bottom of her brokenness, just as I needed him when resting at those church steps.

Oh, how amazed I am when I see his ghostly appearance in the craziest of places: in my brokenness. Never mind the talents of singing, preaching, and writing. Forget about our gifts of intelligence, charm, and beauty. Here we come, Lord, with no abilities, no talents, no entertaining jokes. Just our own torn selves. Our confidence is assured in that he "will not reject a broken and repentant heart" (Ps. 51:17). He simply welcomes us home.

Broke but Close to Home

What is broken is typically shamed. Despicable. Not good enough. When we are not whole, we likely lack confidence in God's ability to use us, mold us, and make us into something better. He seems more like a fairy tale than reality. Thumbing through the Gospels, we see the broken boldly rushing toward him without shame, without hesitation, and even without washing up. There are plenty of scriptural references to people pursuing Jesus with their maimed selves. Funny thing about these broken—they do audacious things in the middle of their desperation.

In Luke 8, Jesus is on his way to the home of Jairus, a leader of the synagogue, whose young daughter is dying. Along the way, crowds mob Jesus. Voices are clamoring for attention. People are pushing left and right, up and down, like drunk groupies at a rock concert trying to get to the stage. A broken woman who has suffered from a bleeding uterus for about twelve years elbow-battles the crowd to try to get to Jesus. Ken Gire, in his book *Intimate Moments with the Savior*, writes of this story in a poignant fashion:

> God only knows how much she's suffered. . . . She has been labeled unclean by the rabbis and subjected to the Levitical prohibitions . . . orphaned by society." And orphaned also by God, or so she thinks. She has prayed. She has pleaded. But for twelve agonizing years God has been silent. . . . She is destitute now. And being out of money, the doctors finally admit there is nothing they can do for her.
>
> Her life is ebbing away. The steady loss of blood over the years has taken its toll. She is anemic, pale, and tired. So very, very tired. . . . She has heard of this physician, this Jesus who comes not to the healthy but to the sick. Who comes not to the strong but to the downtrodden. Who comes not to those with well-ordered lives but to those whose lives are filled with physical and moral chaos. And she has heard of Jesus' success among incurables . . . "Certainly," she thinks, "if I can find this Jesus and but touch the fringe of his garment, I too will be cleansed and made whole."[2]

Brokenness demands of us a type of strength that is impossible when we are complete. It is the strength to admit our imperfections, the crazy desire to touch Christ without bringing too much attention to ourselves, the desire to be whole, to be loved, and to be wrapped in his mercy. Perhaps this brokenness is meant to be a sort of gift. A gift clothed in the ugliest wrapping paper imaginable, yet a gift nonetheless. It comes in every shape and every size and is defined by different circumstances. It's when we hand over our true selves to God, kneeling at his pierced feet and surrendering our brokenness with a smidgen of faith in knowing that he accepts us as we are. More importantly, it's knowing that he loves us and it's not the "I feel so sorry for your pitiful existence" or "I love you because it's my job" type of love.

I find solace that my Savior didn't come simply to applaud people who believe in him and live for him with perfection. He didn't offer his healing touch to those blessed with permanent smiles, chronic joy, and clear skin. He didn't come to comfort those lucky enough not to have "issues," those who don't lug around a three-piece luggage set of hurt and pain. Instead he says, "He has sent me to bind up the brokenhearted" (Isa. 61:1). The book of Psalms offers, "The Lord is close to the brokenhearted and saves those who are crushed in spirit" (Ps. 34:18).

I've often thought it would be unfair to God for us to simply run to him only in moments of grave brokenness. Then I'm reminded of the parable of the prodigal son, a story that most of us are familiar with (see Luke 15:11–32). In his foolish haste, a certain young man spits in his father's face and speeds off toward a life of temporary gratification with the dust of his pride swirling behind him. Though crushed, his father doesn't run after him. He doesn't chase; he doesn't condemn; he doesn't call his son every name in the book. He only stands in the distance, waiting and praying that his boy will come back home, and sooner rather than later.

After some time has passed, the bedraggled silhouette of his son appears on the horizon, and the father's heart leaps with joy. He doesn't murmur under his breath, "Of course the scoundrel would be back. He doesn't have anywhere else to go and hasn't got a darn thing left. Figures he'd come home." No, he runs off to meet him, showers him with hugs and kisses, and clothes him in attire worthy of a prince. His son is home, and that is all that matters.

What I love most about this parable is that this young man's homecoming doesn't necessitate the speech he has probably been preparing. "I screwed up, Dad. I messed up royally. I'm sorry and

I was wrong and . . . and . . . and . . ." The words of an appeal for forgiveness are pointless. What good would a detailed list of sins, wrongs, hurts, and apologies do? The father's boy is finally back home, back in the place he needed and was needed most.

There is a prodigal son in all of us. A form of brokenness that causes us to come to our Father with our hearts in our throats. Words seem pointless. We may be ashamed of the things we've done wrong, we may feel the dominating pain of losing someone, we may have experienced a circumstance that leaves us hopeless. Whatever it is, we're there at his feet. It doesn't matter how long it took us or how we decided to come to him; the fact is, we've come home. I believe that is the greatest gift we can give our Father. Our broken spirits . . . ourselves.

True, sometimes it may not seem to be the most noble of things. Sometimes running to God is the only item on our list we haven't crossed off yet. Perhaps it would have served us best if we came to him first or held on to him longer so we wouldn't be consumed with our brokenness. Yes, I admit that sometimes it's only after my kicking and screaming, after the tantrum-throwing and flinging of accusations toward God, that I realize I'm left with him as my final but best option. It's with a shamed heart and timid spirit that I cock an eye upward, pray for forgiveness, and seek him. I don't believe he rolls his eyes and with a sarcastic sneer says, "Well, A. J., my goodness, it's about time." No. I believe he takes my face in his hands, wipes the tears away, and whispers, "I'm glad you decided to come. I've been waiting for you."

This is what has left me clinging to the Christian faith as long as I have, despite my many past prayerful threats to become an atheist or agnostic. I used to continually torment myself about not being good enough and crush whatever good spirit I had because I wasn't perfect . . . because everyone said I looked wild . . . and because I'd rather worship God on the beach by myself than in church with a bunch of people who wear pastel cardigan sets, flowery dresses, and trendy button-downs. But the One who saved me doesn't mind my brokenness, my idiosyncrasies, or even my seemingly irreverent prayers. Being broken is certainly not the best thing in the world to be, but it doesn't make us terrible human beings or lost causes. Sometimes it simply affords us a way to come home. And usually this type of acceptance is what can make us stay there.

6

IS GOD GOING TO
TAKE CARE OF ME?

I am still confident of this: I will see the goodness of the LORD in
the land of the living.

Psalm 27:13

What do you think of when you hear the question, "Is God going
to take care of me?" It means something different to different
people and can be asked in more specific ways: "Is God going to
answer my prayers?" "Is he going to satisfy my desires?" "Is he
going to fulfill my dreams?" "Is he going to pull through for me?"
"Is he going to give me what I want, what I need, or what I think
I want or need?" Trying to find the answers to these questions
can be quite a Herculean task, especially if you are equidistant
between saying yes or no, when you are stuck in the middle, hop-

ing beyond hope that the answer is yes but being drawn toward no by the gravitational pull of fear or doubt.

As small group leaders, my friend and I begin each meeting by taking prayer requests. We get all kinds. Some ask for prayer for traveling mercies for an upcoming trip. Some ask for success for a job interview. Some ask for healing. Some ask for recovery from an addiction. Week after week, we ask if we can pray for whatever it is they need. And week after week, hands are raised, requests are uttered, we proclaim our belief that God will answer their prayers, and we pray.

I often think about the people who jostle with doubt as we pray. I'm not clairvoyant and I don't think I have the spiritual gift of discernment to be able to see through or read people like the daily paper. Yet I can't help but recognize a familiar wince in the eyes of some people every once in a while when we talk about God answering prayer, meeting needs, and being faithful. I see it when the conversation more or less gets rerouted in the direction of the question, "Is God going to take care of us?"

Having been in their shoes, I know their confidence in God is at least somewhat deflated. And who am I to tell them to blow it back up right then and there? I certainly don't know the intricate details of their lives, and I don't know if they even want me to know. I know they labor with unresolved issues and probably even unanswerable questions. I know they numbly stare at my co-leader and me as we spout off Christianese verbiage that I can't help but think sometimes echoes the childlike overtone of a nursery rhyme.

We've all heard this type of lingo before, when some religious elite takes a passage from the Bible, pours some sugary sweet maple syrup over it, and attempts to encourage us with their naive commentary. I'll use the words of Jesus in Matthew 6 as an example. This is what he communicated:

Look at the birds. They don't plant or harvest or store food in barns, for your heavenly Father feeds them. And aren't you far more valuable to him than they are? Can all your worries add a single moment to your life? And why worry about your clothing? Look at the lilies of the field and how they grow. They don't work or make their clothing, yet Solomon in all his glory was not dressed as beautifully as they are. And if God cares so wonderfully for wildflowers that are here today and thrown into the fire tomorrow, he will certainly care for you. Why do you have so little faith? So don't worry about these things, saying, "What will we eat? What will we drink? What will we wear?" . . . Your heavenly Father already knows all your needs. Seek the Kingdom of God above all else, and live righteously, and he will give you everything you need.

Matthew 6:26–33 NLT

The naive editorial goes something like this: "God loves you. He sure does. He takes care of every lily in the field. See them swaying in the soft summer breeze? Well, they're not concerned about what they're wearing because they know God will take care of them. See the bird that just flew into the kitchen window? Well, he may be klutzy, but he's definitely not worried about whether or not he's going to have food on the table tomorrow. The Bible says that he gets his meals catered by God. So why should you worry then? Why should you allow yourself to be unnecessarily burdened by wondering if God is going to take care of you? The birds, the flowers—all are absent of anxiety. They enjoy life. They trust in God with childlike ease, practically without even thinking about it. Relax, take it easy. Everything is going to be just fine." (Insert saccharine smile.)

This has an element of truth to it, but it doesn't connect with most people who live in the middle of stark realities. Why? It seems preposterous to compare the apparel needs of a flower with legitimate needs of survival and even with the burdens that come from unspeakable tragedies. Do lilies have mortgages? Do lilies have to survive only on food stamps? Do lilies have to work three jobs to single-handedly support two small kids? Do birds get cheated on and publicly humiliated by their spouse? Are birds tempted by the lure of painkillers? Do birds watch, helpless and heartbroken, as their children die from an incurable disease? This is what we who are so desperate for a deep, not naive, faith are thinking.

When I read the words of Jesus, I am appreciative of the lesson in simplicity he offered. But I also think he was alluding to a basic but profound truth that we need to remind ourselves of. I doubt he was referring to human anxieties born from such frivolous tasks as finding the perfect outfit for our company holiday party or trying to decide if we should have sushi or pizza for lunch. I don't think he was simply juxtaposing the needs of plants and animals with our own life complexities. He was saying that we matter to him. That he cares.

Sometimes what "Will God take care of me?" really means is "Does God even care?" Isn't that what most believers want to know? Something happens when we get so caught up in religiosity; in numbly saying and doing the right things; in preaching to ourselves the lessons that were ingrained in our young minds in Sunday school; and in responding to what we suppose are stupid questions with flat Christian lingo and pat, cookie-cutter answers. We stop being honest. We stop admitting that we have legitimate questions we need to ask. God forbid we should ever wonder if God cares about us. Some people would accuse us of committing heresy.

I know people ask that question, though, including myself. So did the disciples of Jesus, and they were the ones who shared such an intimate and unique relationship with Christ. They walked and talked with him. They watched him open the eyes of the blind and straighten crooked limbs. They were front-row witnesses to the supernatural in action, but let me tell you, when they found themselves in the absence of his literal presence and facing what felt like intentional abandonment, even they panicked. Their picture of Christ as their twenty-four-hour bodyguard and protector from trouble started to fizzle out of their imagination.

The New Testament records the famous story of Jesus feeding five thousand people with a meager five loaves of bread and two fish. On this day Jesus not only performs an incredible miracle in satisfying the growling stomachs of a massive crowd but also serves them in different ways before they were fed. Mark tells us that Jesus "had compassion on them, because they were like sheep without a shepherd" (Mark 6:34). He talks to them. He shares with them heavenly wisdom. He scoops up little children in his hands and blesses them. He even heals people.

The whole scene is quite a revival. I bet you anything this is a very proud moment for the disciples. The twelve are probably tickled pink (or something more manly) at being such an integral part of the ministry of the prophesied Messiah. Beaming and proud, they watch as people hungry for understanding are fed with truth. As broken people become whole. As starved people become full.

But then, out of nowhere, the scene and the spine-tingling energy completely shift. Doesn't this sound familiar? Ever experience a time of transcendent spirituality or a period when life is relatively trauma-free and breezy, and then all of a sudden, in an inexplicable moment, your sense of security is lost and your bubble of joy bursts? Doesn't it seem in those moments that God almost purposefully turns the tables around, cocks his head in our direction, and waits to see our reaction as a result of this about-face? It feels almost bipolar.

Well, something like that happens here. Just as the disciples are rubbing their bellies in satisfaction and thinking they probably shouldn't have eaten that third roll, Jesus does something strange. He tells them to leave—without him. Some translations say Jesus "made" (NIV) them go or "insisted" (NLT) that they get in the boat and head over "to the other side" of the lake (Matt. 14:22). Either way, you get the feeling they don't want to go. I'm sure they beg Jesus to let them stay. After all, the party is just getting started. The disciples are having a great time—a spiritually great time. Good things are happening. Nobody is getting gratified in a selfish, indulgent, or sinful sense. God is working through his Son, and everybody is getting something out of it. Why would party-pooper Jesus want them to leave?

But he makes them go. He forces them into the boat while he stays by himself to pray, which is definitely a worthy and necessary thing for Jesus to do. So while Jesus is meditating and the disciples are paddling toward the other side, hemming and hawing about Jesus leaving them alone and muttering God-only-knows-what under their fishy breath, things get even worse.

The winds start blowing, the rain starts pouring, and the waves start climbing. This is no twenty-minute squall that disappears as quickly as it appears. This continues for hours. It starts sometime in the evening and persists until "the fourth watch of the night" (Matt. 14:25), which is anywhere between three and six in the morning. So for almost an entire night, these poor men are tossed about on the violent waves like a rag doll in the mouth of a Rottweiler. We can guess, probably with much accuracy, what they were thinking.

"I can't believe this!" "How could Jesus have left us?" "Why did he make us ride in a storm?" "Where is he when we need him?"

"Is he coming back?" "Is he going to save us?" I'd venture to guess even a few "bleepity-bleepity-bleeps" slipped out.

Is God going to take care of me?

So many Christians experience the depth of their spirituality in terms of mountaintop experiences, miracles, or smooth-sailing times. They become almost intoxicated with having everything work out in all ways at all times. Maybe they are smart enough or rich enough or pretty enough or important enough to satisfy their own needs without the providence of God. Maybe they are spiritual enough to procure answers to every prayer. Maybe they are wise enough to not get bogged down by temporal circumstances and to maintain emotional and mental stability all the time. Most of us aren't.

Here we have the trusty disciples of Jesus who only hours earlier stood shoulder-to-shoulder with their Master as he miraculously supplied the human needs of a wanting, sick, and hungry crowd. And now they are being thrashed about by wind, rain, and waves and belting out, "Is he going to take care of us?" They clearly knew he had the capacity to do so. I bet they were overwhelmed not just in wondering if Jesus was going to save them but because of the distressing fact that he had sent them into the storm. It's kind of brutal, isn't it? Did he really care about them that much when he basically bulldozed them out of the festivities only for them to get drenched and pummeled by a storm? Did he really care about them that much when he waited until the fourth watch, almost the very last second, to show up?

The story ends with Jesus coming to them walking on the water. Overcome by fear, they start to freak out. Maybe they see something that looks like Casper the Friendly Ghost or, worse, Ebenezer Scrooge's Ghost of Christmas Yet to Come. Either way, Jesus comes, but in their estimation, he was late. They weren't sure why he had sent them in the first place. It felt dreadful to be battling rains and winds and waves in the absence of his presence. But finally, he comes.

"Is God going to take care of us?" is the cry that resonates from most of us caught in senseless storms. It doesn't mean you are a faithless Christian. It doesn't mean that you are not smart enough to trust him. It doesn't mean whatever negative thing the super-Christian will say you are because you are even asking such a seemingly silly question. It just means that you are asking it. That you wonder. And that you have no choice but to hold on so you can experience the affirmative answer. You stay in the boat and wait for Jesus to come. You may end up like Peter, walking on the water with him, or like the other disciples, sitting in the boat. Sitting, standing, rowing, walking, wading, whatever you are doing, know this: Jesus always comes.

Belief and Unbelief—A Love Affair

For a long time I was plagued with a question I relied on others to answer. I found myself at the end of the same rope I'd climbed a dozen times before. The rope was falling apart. The braided fibers were loose, and the edges were embarrassingly frayed. But there I was, hanging on for dear life while slowly slipping down.

"Am I going to be okay?" I called my sister, my sister-in-law, and my best friend more times than I'd care to even admit. Time and time again they would laugh and tell me the same thing in different ways. "Of course you are, A. J. You are going to be just fine." For five minutes their reassurance would make me feel better. Safe. Confident. Cool and collected. But at minute six, the shadows loomed. I rolled my eyes and told myself, "Fine? You are going to be fine? Are you kidding me? What are you? Nuts? Of course you are not going to be fine!"

Sigh.

My poor friends. No matter how eloquently spoken or sincere their confidence, it didn't absolve me of anxiety, so I repeated the question a gazillion times. I was becoming quite pathetic. Eventually I realized I had to stop asking. Not because my spirit was satisfied with their answers but because my questioning was annoying for them to hear.

The better question I was asking, though I did not fully recognize it at the time, was "Is God going to take care of me?" I can honestly say that for a few good years, I didn't know for certain. There I was trying to overcome an addiction that only 60 percent of women recover from with treatment. I had watched all my friends find their soul mates while I found myself alone, year after year. My finances never seemed to gain any stability, and paying some bills was a battle most of the time. The book rejections were piling up. My depression had attached itself to me like fungus; no reprieve seemed to be in sight, and while Prozac and other medication helped to stabilize my erratic mood swings, I found myself playing GI Jane to stay somewhat sane and normal. I would force myself to pretend I was okay. I laughed. I smiled. I told funny jokes. The refuse littered under my phony smile and forced giggles remained invisible to everyone except me. I made myself rejoice in the blessings and answered prayers of others. Hallelujah. Praise the Lord. Amen.

"Is God going to take care of me?" Who knew? At one point I sought the answer to this question in a charismatic church. It made perfect sense. Charismatics were loud, they were exciting, they were happy, and it seemed that whoever signed a membership card to a faith-focused church always got what they wanted, whether a husband, a fancy car, or a really good parking space.

Before all you word-of-faith people start clubbing me with your Bibles, let me say that I love these kinds of churches. I really do. Every now and then I visit one that's near my home because I love the energy and the positivism and I know I'll get blessed every time. Please allow me the space to share my experience without thinking I am crucifying a particular denomination.

Week after week and sometimes even a couple times a week, I found myself planted on the pews of this contagiously spirited church. I listened to sermons on tape several times a day and joined a new members class. As I continued to engage in this optimistic environment with much devotion, here is what happened: I developed a more positive, victorious attitude. I got happy and excited. The thirty Post-it notes I slapped on my bathroom mirror reminding me of promises found in Scripture especially helped. Repeating "I'm blessed, not stressed" after my car broke down, or my boss yelled at me, or I had impossible deadlines, or I was a bad daughter again might have helped too.

Eventually, however, the newfound energy waned. My buzz faded. It was terrible! I felt like the antithesis of what my church represented. I had transformed into an official faux champion with a cheap costume that was starting to tear in all the wrong places. I still wasn't entirely sure if God was going to take care of me. I had just sprinkled the question with fairy dust and pretended, "Well, duh, of course!"

But over the course of time, my spirit switched into a better, more balanced gear. I got candid about my doubt and simultaneously started to understand that even in the moments of uncertainty, somehow God would take care of me. Believe it or not, I had even felt this way when I had stopped going to church for a time. In hindsight, this coupling of belief and honest unbelief was what led me to the path of ultimate surrender and transformation.

Recently I flipped through the journal I had kept since 2002. I'm not a consistent journaler, by any means. I get nervous when somebody gives me a pretty diary because I know the minute I write just the date in my chicken scratch, the pretty diary will cease being pretty. Yet for some reason during these years of wondering, I tirelessly wrote. I scribbled pages and pages about the angst of whether or not my life was going to turn out okay and questioning whether all the demons that picked, poked, and prodded at my thin skin would ever leave me alone.

Here is what I wrote many, many years ago, when I was relentlessly pressing into faith, when I was crawling out of my hole by the grace and the faith given to me by God himself:

I struggled for the past two days. With sadness. And also going to the toilet with intent to puke up my food and saying no. Or more like, "No, no, it's not worth it." . . . My new mantra is repeating, "I believe in the God who will give me the desires of my heart." Sometimes I chant it with an overwhelming faith and it brings tears to my eyes, and other times I say it while the dueling thoughts of faith and fear duke it out on the battlefront. . . . What do I believe today? I do believe in the God who will give me the desires of my heart. But maybe like 40 percent. It's better than the 1 percent I had two nights ago. . . .

I've got no answers, a blurred vision, and apparently someone by my side. That is what I believe with my whole heart. I believe that he is sitting on my bed, the intangible-invisible, as I write with nonsensical fury, and he is probably giggling at my wordiness. And he is probably thinking, "You're going to laugh one day, A. J. You're going to laugh and smile and dance and shout. And you're going to trust me, and you're going to know that I AM the God who will give you the desires of your heart. That your faith does not go unnoticed, whether it's 1 percent or 99 percent. That I don't view your addictions as stumbling blocks that would prevent me to move in you. I want you to live, shout, dance . . . with the freedom that I gave you . . . that I want you to have."

And that is what I believe. It sounds like a fairy tale, or like a Saturday morning cartoon. But I like this fairy tale, because it keeps my faith moving like ants in the pants (Buechner) . . . it gives me wonder, and marvel, and mystery. It makes my heart leap with joy for no reason and forms a lump in my throat for the same reason. . . .

Lord, I don't know what I'm doing, and I admit there are addictions in my life, but I love you and want to continue to trust you . . . whether 1 percent or 99 percent. Right now, my faith has been bumped to 70 percent. You never fail to amaze me. You never fail to surprise me. You never fail to amuse me. You never fail to make my heart leap. I love you. And I believe that you—the God I believe who will give me the desires of my heart—love me more than I can ever imagine.

I wrote more entries like this. What was going on? I wanted to grasp that I would eventually be okay. I wanted to believe that God would take care of me. For me, what this meant was that I would one day be free from a painful addiction and the thick residue of its emotional, mental, and physical side effects. That I would get the desires of my heart—the desires that I believed God had given me. That I would live resting in ultimate peace. That I would, as the psalmist voiced, "see the LORD's goodness while I am here in the land of the living" (Ps. 27:13 NLT).

In essence, my theme prayer was, "I believe, Lord. I believe sometimes a little, sometimes a lot. I know you are going to take care of me. Or at least I believe more than I don't believe. At least for today." My faith wasn't absolute by any stretch. Piggybacking my hopeful fervor was the statement recorded in Mark from the wise father: "I do believe; help me overcome my unbelief" (Mark 9:24, emphasis added).

I came to the point where I had to stop relying on stuff, on people, on religion, and on cute inspirational phrases to provide me with interim comfort. I had to get honest, throw my hands up in surrender, and push through the question instead of letting it rule my sanity or influence my relationship with God. I had to believe in God, in his goodness, in his power, and in his love. I had to trust and hope, even and especially in the presence of my mess, acknowledging the not-so-perfect in my life but believing anyway that he would somehow make things beautiful.

As time went on, I developed a better and sweeter assurance in him. I'm telling you, it wasn't because of a positive change in my circumstances. That was one of the greatest lessons I learned during this time. It's so easy to trust in God when things are looking up, isn't it? But it's a different thing entirely to trust him when you don't have much to show for it and when your doubt keeps popping into your head like an annoying in-law.

Here's an example. I wrote the following journal entry after an excruciating breakup with a boyfriend. At the time I was not getting any writing jobs and even thought my career was officially kaput after I got horrible feedback from a potential client. A good part of me was depressed and lost and wondering and wandering, but another part of me remained hopeful. Hopeful for literally God-knew-what. I wrote,

> Hope is a very mysterious thing, and I'll go so far as to say that it usually goes against our nature. Especially in times of trouble. Especially when our track record in a certain situation has proved futile in the past. But the worst thing to do is to let go of faith. To allow our emotions, our circumstances, the opinions of our friends

and mentors to turn hope into dust. Apathy. Nothing. Instead of grasping at straws—which is something of what hope usually looks like—we fold our arms in surrender and say things like *"que sera, sera,"* "whatever," "there is nothing I can do about it." But there is—believe.

When the forces of evil, or happenstance, or simply life are clawing at your sanity, telling you that all is lost . . . all is forsaken . . . all means nothing, when well-intentioned friends just tell you to give up and move on in indifference, when your alter ego is whispering in your ear to numb your feelings in ways that will ultimately end up destroying your integrity or a semblance of peace—believe instead.

Believe for what you want to believe. Believe in the impossible. Believe in the forsaken, forgotten dreams or desires. Believe that today you can get a phone call that will change your life. Or that the knock on your door this afternoon can turn your situation around in such a whirlwind of a way that you will feel sheepish not to have believed more. Or that you'll meet someone with the power to set your destiny on a different, more fulfilling course.

I always believe because I just can't not believe. Sometimes it's not so noble. Some might say it's a little foolish. But I can't help it. I believe because I want a better future. Because I want dreams to come true. Because I love the magic in seeing God work in ways that I know I could never dream of figuring out myself. Lord, I believe; help me with my unbelief.

I don't know the formula for believing in times of doubt except to do it and pray that God, through his Spirit, will give us the faith to keep believing however much we can in that moment, because the Bible teaches us that even faith is a gift from him. Believing that God will take care of you when you feel like he isn't or he won't doesn't always look so polished, clean, or put-together. I just know that part of the mystery of God is that he can, with X-ray vision, see straight through the rat's nest of our souls to the beauty of our desperate faith.

"Is God going to take care of me?" When you lay your head on your pillow tonight, the lights are off, and your realities are screaming louder than the bleating sheep you're trying to count, think of the answer you will give. If you can't reply with a resounding yes just yet, you can simply allow the faith and doubt that's clamoring for your attention to clasp hands and walk down the path together. Answer the question honestly: "My God, my God, I honestly don't know if you'll take care of me. I think you will. No, I hope you will. I'm going to believe you will. Somehow. Lord, I do believe. But help me overcome my unbelief."

Enough Already

The question of this chapter makes me think about the early Israelites. For over two centuries this group of people lived in Egypt, a nation commonly referred to in the Bible as "the land of slavery" (Exod. 13:3). Although the Israelites were once recognized as champions, they had become slaves in a foreign land. Many of you are familiar with the exodus story, told in Exodus 3–14, thanks in part to Charlton Heston or Sunday school.

Moses, though an unlikely candidate, is chosen to lead the people of Israel out of bondage and out of Egypt. Through the glowing flames of a burning bush in a desert, God shocks the sandals off of the elderly Moses and charges him with a daunting task. He orders Moses to approach Pharaoh in his golden palace and demand, as the famous line goes, that the oppressive leader of Egypt "Let God's people go." After Moses tap dances around God's divine commission and enumerates the considerable amount of flaws and inabilities that he imagines would preclude him from being successful at this task, he finally says, "Okay."

Moses then, on several occasions, pleads with Pharaoh to release the Jewish slaves, but Pharaoh refuses. He doesn't budge. There is no obvious room for compromise, so Moses threatens that the Lord will send horrible plagues upon the people of Egypt. A stubborn Pharaoh rolls his eyes and basically remarks, "Yeah, yeah, yeah. Big whoop-de-friggin'-do. What do I care? I will not let you guys out of here." Despite the grotesque and deadly plagues of locusts, frogs, pestilence, boils, and waters of blood, the Israelites remain captive, their wrists and ankles adorned with shiny Egyptian shackles. That is, until the final plague is cast and the firstborn of every household is killed, including Pharaoh's own son. This gets his blood pumping, and he practically kicks Moses and the Israelites out of his kingdom, barking, "Go on, get out of here! Don't let the gates hit you on the way out. And for heaven's sake, don't come back!"

The Israelites, free after over four hundred years of being treated more like animals than human beings, hit the ground running, right on the heels of their fierce leader, Moses. But only a few days later, something sobers Pharaoh and he realizes—with a Homer Simpson "D'oh!"—that he had just booted millions of good workhorses out of his kingdom. Magnificent army in tow, Pharaoh races to catch up with the Jewish people to force them back into captivity.

What follows is one of the most spectacular miracles in the exodus story—the parting of the Red Sea. Before the phenomenon, however, the Israelites are sandwiched between two formidable adversaries: an army and a sea. From the looks of things, their exodus victory is likely to be short-lived. "You have got to be kidding," they say. "This is ridiculous. A sick joke!" They deliver the first bout of their infamous string of complaints and murmurs. They cry their agony to Moses, who was once regarded as their fearless defender but is now looking and feeling more like a thorn in their side—or at least like a leader who doesn't know what the heck he's doing. "Why did you bring us out here to die in the wilderness? Weren't there enough graves for us in Egypt? What have you done to us? Why did you make us leave Egypt? Didn't we tell you this would happen while we were still in Egypt? We said, 'Leave us alone! Let us be slaves to the Egyptians. It's better to be a slave in Egypt than a corpse in the wilderness!'" (Exod. 14:11–12 NLT).

They don't even bother asking God to get them out of this jam; they just assume he won't. So the Israelites do what they know best to do. They reach into their past and pull out whatever is comfortable, easier, and less work. "Give us our binding chains," they demand. "Let us wear our slave clothes again. Send us back into captivity. It's got to be better than dying like this." Moses encourages them not to be afraid and voices his confidence that the Lord will deliver them.

What I find so interesting is what God says to Moses after Moses gives the people a short but inspiring speech: "Why are you crying out to me? Tell the people to get moving!" (Exod. 14:15 NLT). It is as though God is somewhat aloof in his reaction to their discouragement and ear-splitting wailing because he already knows he is going to pull through, and in quite an epic fashion, no less. I think God must have thought that these men and women were acting like drama queens, like when a five-year-old child mildly stubs her toe on the playground and screams like a banshee, as if it's the end of the world.

But what happens to the nation of Israel as they watch, with white knuckles and beads of sweat pouring down their faces, as the army of their enemy closes in on them from behind? The Red Sea miraculously parts, the Israelites mosey on through, and just as the wheels of the front line of chariots touch down on the dry shoreline, the walls of water crash down and drown the entire Egyptian army. This incredible incident prompts the nation of Israel to "put their faith in the LORD" (Exod. 14:31 NLT). Would God take care of them? If you went around their camp that day and submitted the question to random people, most everyone would have said, "Yes!" in booming, victorious voices coated with lots of confidence.

Fast-forward to a few days later when the Israelites find themselves without drinkable water. The only water to be found is bitter and tastes like metal. So they complain and groan and stamp their dirty, sandaled feet in frustration. (Granted, I know it's not pleasant to be dehydrated, and I can imagine the parents must have been quite concerned for their children.) Moses shuts them up with another promise from God and performs another miracle. At God's instruction, Moses throws a piece of wood into the bitter water, and it turns into sweet, refreshing drink. The Israelites once again put on their happy faces and dance around the miracle springs.

About a month later, they run out of food. Are you thinking what I'm thinking? God had consistently shown his faithfulness to them in supernatural ways. Every time prior that they found themselves in a tight spot, a way was always provided for them to squeeze through. So surely this time they would not yap their complaints but peacefully rely on God to do something, right? Wrong. The Israelites find the old scripts they had tossed in garbage cans and start reciting the same old lines. "'If only the Lord had killed us back in Egypt,' they moaned. 'There we sat around pots filled with meat and ate all the bread we wanted. But now you have brought us into this wilderness to starve us all to death'" (Exod. 16:3 NLT).

See the pattern? I am in no way making a harsh example out of these people, because as you remember, I really do relate to them. Plus, if I, or for that matter you, were in their shoes, do we really know for certain how we would think, feel, or act? Let's be honest. We all experience some measure of anxiety when we're hit with life circumstances out of our control. A little fear or worry or wonder is normal. Of this I'm positive. But by the same token, it would do us good to pause and reflect on how God has taken care of us this far, to remember the work of his hands in the past, and to repeat the mantra that, "Yes, he has taken care of us before, and he will certainly do it again." True, sometimes that leap of faith can feel like a more menacing opponent than a Red Sea or an Egyptian army. But this was a lesson that would have served the Israelites well and one that we need to learn today.

After the Jewish people experience their initial deliverance and their thirst is quenched, God makes sure that during their entire forty-year sojourn, they never go hungry. He feeds them with manna every single day (see Exod. 16:35). Yet they don't stop complaining during their wandering in the wilderness. Every now and then some schmuck pipes up, "For Pete's sake, Moses, why did you send us out here to die?" And until they receive whatever it is they need or want, they beg Moses to take them back to Egypt, a land they have falsely painted as paradise.

How often do we do things like that? We refuse to rest in God's presence until we are satisfied by his provision. Do you find yourself saying things like this to him: "Why on earth did I choose to follow you when all you did is lead me into a storm?" "Why did I put my trust in you when you took me the long way into my future, through a barren wasteland?" "You are clearly not taking care of me. I should have pledged allegiance to myself, to my parents, to

135

my boss, to my husband, to my rich uncle, to my professor, or to my own intuition, hard work, and intelligence, instead of you." Is God going to take care of us? He is. He really, really is. Usually it's not in the way that we would have designed, however. We have no formula or blueprint for how he will lead us out of storms or through deserts. The only thing he asks of us is to trust in him. When uncertainty temporarily clouds your faith and you wrestle with that question, remember God's words to Moses: "Why are you crying out to me? Tell the people to get moving!" (Exod. 14:15 NLT). Don't stop. Keep moving. Keep your faith active. Believe and have confidence that we will see the goodness of God manifested in our present lives.

We must all get to the point where enough is enough. Where the question stops carrying such an overwhelming weight that it drags us down. I don't know where that point is for you, and you don't know where it is for me. But I believe if we rest in relationship with him, if we cling to his presence, if we remember his promises, and if we reflect on the provisions of yesterday, then we get a step closer to voicing a "Yes." We really must be satisfied with his presence alone—whether or not we feel it—as we wait on the "taking care of" part.

The prophet Jeremiah said, "Blessed are those who trust in the LORD and have made the LORD their hope and confidence" (Jer. 17:7 NLT). Blessed are we when we are stranded in downpours, when we are hungry, when we are thirsty, when we have an enemy lurking so close we can smell his stank breath, but we nonetheless trust in God to take care of us, his children. Oh, how incredibly blessed are we to even have that option.

7

FORGIVE US . . .
AS WE FORGIVE OTHERS

Forgiveness is the fragrance that the violet sheds on the heel that
has crushed it.

Mark Twain

Thirty-two-year-old truck driver Charlie Roberts was a tormented
man. But nobody really knew the extent of his internal agony, not
even his own wife. He had harbored an ugly secret for the past
twenty years. He had sexually molested two young relatives, and
the perverse thought of doing it again saturated his mind since
that day. Apparently no one else knew of the crime, but Charlie
did, and it was enough to ultimately ravage his sense of sanity and
his moral compass.

He tried living a normal life. He got married, he kept steady jobs,
and he and his wife even had children, one of whom, named Elise,

died at birth. Perhaps this was the icing on the proverbial cake, a tragedy that Charlie had never been able to accept or deal with in an appropriate manner. Some who knew him saw no evidence of violence; others called him a troubled soul. Either way, his private hell existed, and the facade of normalcy eventually shattered on October 2, 2006.

Armed with an arsenal of a 9mm handgun, a 12-gauge shotgun, a .30-06 bolt-action rifle, about 600 rounds of ammunition, cans of black powder, a stun gun, two knives, a change of clothes, sexual lubricant, what seemed to be a truss board, and a box containing a hammer, hacksaw, pliers, wire, screws, bolts, and tape, Charlie stormed into an Amish schoolhouse in Pennsylvania and allowed evil to take possession of that morning. He released fifteen male students, a pregnant teacher, and three parents with small children. Then he barricaded the doors and forced the remaining students to line up against a chalkboard. Those ten girls stood in row formation, shuddering, crying, wrought with fear, and paralyzed by whatever their imagination led them to believe would happen to them.

Around this time, Charlie's wife got home from a prayer meeting to find four suicide notes scattered on a table. One was addressed to her; the others were written to their three children. Her letter contained these words: "I don't know how you put up with me all these years. I am not worthy of you. You are the perfect wife. You deserve so much better. We had so many good memories together as well as the tragedy with Elise. It changed my life forever. I haven't been the same since. It affected me in a way I never felt possible. I am filled with so much hate—hate towards myself, hate towards God, and unimaginable emptiness. It seems like every time we do something fun, I think about how Elise wasn't here to share it with us and go right back to anger." The note also exposed his "dreams of molesting again."

Torn with disbelief and confusion, his wife immediately dialed 911, and state troopers and members of the Amish community began to arrive at the tiny, one-room schoolhouse. A large crowd gathered, and the officers ordered Charlie to exit the building. Their intervention proved unsuccessful; twenty minutes later, he started shooting the victims at point-blank range. Three girls died at the scene, two died in a hospital the next morning, and five others were seriously injured. Charlie ended the siege by killing himself. The deputy coroner observed one child with twenty bullet wounds and stated there wasn't even a space in that school room that wasn't splattered with blood.

Before the blood had an opportunity to dry and with its distinct metallic odor permeating the air, the Amish community extended a grace that many of us would consider unfathomable. This group of people became breathing examples of an indescribable forgiveness that some of us, in the depths of our hearts, may feel was even inappropriate in the magnifying light of such a gruesome evil. The Amish extol the virtue and act of forgiveness. This may seem an easy thing to advocate, especially in the absence of an experience that mandates the call for its practice. But the Amish community did forgive, and only, I believe, through their faith in a God who has forgiveness in his very core of being.

On the day of the murder, a grandfather of one of the victims made this shocking statement: "We must not think evil of this man."[1] Another member of the Amish community said, "I don't think there's anybody here that wants to do anything but forgive and not only reach out to those who have suffered a loss in that way but to reach out to the family of the man who committed these acts."[2] Some folks compassionately set up a memorial fund for Charlie's widow and three children. Several of the victims' parents even attended his funeral, a vivid expression of the extension of grace. At the cemetery, they embraced the widow of the man who had violently ended the lives of their innocent girls for reasons no one could comprehend. This group of people refused to be overwhelmed by the outpouring of their own cup of suffering and instead looked into the eyes of the killer's wife and said, "We forgive."

It is a principle they live by. It is a grace they understand. And while they didn't make light of the tragedy, or ignore the severity of the crime, or callously stop the river of tears that flooded their eyes but were fully aware that mourning would run its twisted and winding course, they engaged in what they felt they were called to do: forgive. In a way I completely do not understand, they recognized that rebuilding could only begin from the depths of a forgiving spirit. That's a place that some of us avoid for a myriad of reasons.

As for the rest of the world who watched the news and read the articles revealing this act of extraordinary forgiveness, we remained glued to the reports with a numbing shock. I know many of us were pummeled by a wave of humility. When I saw the headlines that blared the reality of forgiveness, I burst into tears. I don't have children and honestly have not been in a situation where I have endured an incredible physical or emotional offense and had to bite my lip, swallow my pride, and utter the words, "I forgive you." But it brought to my attention the power of forgiveness. And it made me wonder if I could follow in the footsteps of this remarkable community if the situation ever called for it. I'd like to think that I would, but honestly . . . would I? I don't know.

I know stories of people who have suffered at the hands of inconceivable evil and have survived only through the healing of being able to forgive their offender. And I know plenty of other stories of people in the same position who have refused to offer such grace and have allowed the pain to fester and transform into bitterness, a concrete wall that prevented them from experiencing the freedom found in forgiving. What is it exactly that creates the space for grace to move into forgiveness?

Jesus taught us, "And when you stand praying, if you hold anything against anyone, forgive him, so that your Father in heaven may forgive you your sins" (Mark 11:25). How often are we so desperate to be forgiven by God? How often do we whisper begging prayers to be shown mercy and grace by the Almighty? How often do we mess up in our lives only to rest in the confidence and security that he will forgive us of all our sins—the small ones and the big ones? And how often do we hold grudges against people who hurt us, lie to us, criticize us, gossip about us, say mean things to us, deceive us, are malicious to us, and wantonly hurt us? This is an imbalance that many of us have tremendous difficulty in straightening out.

I know a woman who has held a grudge against someone for the past twenty years. A relative of hers had said some pretty nasty things about the relationship between her and her spouse. And for two decades this woman held on to the offense for dear life. There was no sermon, no wise counsel, no common sense, no teaching, and especially no command from Jesus that would nudge her toward finding a space of grace for that man. She spent those years cradling and even nurturing the hurt and made it clear even to this man's children that he had hurt her and she would never offer forgiveness . . . even though he repeatedly begged for it with a humble desperation. This bitterness clung to her like asbestos, and if she found herself in the same room with him, she would leave—after she threw him an evil glance reminding him, I suppose, of his wrongs.

Recently he asked me to intervene. It saddened me for many reasons, one of them being that I knew it was impossible for me to say anything that would remedy the situation. With tears welling up in his eyes, he kneeled in front of me on the cold, hard pavement, clasped his calloused hands together, and said, "A. J., if she would let me, I would bow before her on my hands and knees just like I'm doing now and beg for forgiveness." I felt so incredibly sorry for him. And I knew that unless God's grace penetrated her envenomed soul and the truth of his mercy could chisel away at her hurts, nothing could be done.

Holding on to grievances does nothing beneficial for us. The sixteenth-century Carmelite mystic, Saint John of the Cross, wrote, "Attachment to a hurt arising from a past event blocks the inflow of hope into our lives."[3] Henri Nouwen, a Dutch Catholic priest, once said, "By not forgiving I chain myself to a desire to get even, thereby losing my freedom."[4] Jesus was fully aware of the potency of unforgiveness, and that is why he advocated the practice of forgiving. He knew that lugging around any weight of resentment creates an emotional and spiritual block. It binds people. It haunts them. It even makes them physically sick.

Once Peter, one of Jesus's disciples, asked Jesus how many times we are required to forgive those who offend us. Peter thought he had hit an epiphany and asked his Master, "Seven times? Should we forgive people seven times?" Jesus answered, "I tell you, not seven times, but seventy-seven times" (Matt. 18:22)—in other words, an infinite number of times.

I know some of you have suffered horrible experiences at the hands of misinformed or foolish people or even faced pure evil. People do wicked things sometimes, whether from selfish motives, out of mental illness, or simply just because. I think of innocent kids who have been physically, emotionally, and sexually violated by people who were entrusted to care and love them. I think of women who have been brutally raped. I think of children who have swindled money from their parents. I think of spouses who have purposely destroyed the precious bond of marriage with infidelity and lies.

I'm not saying that you should be best friends with your offender or are under a moral obligation to maintain a relational connection with those who have hurt you. Boundaries are necessary; of this I am well aware. Space is appropriate to protect yourself from those who wish ill on you. Still, we are called to forgive. Many times those who have wronged us will not ask to be forgiven, but we are still required to find a place in our hearts to offer it to them. And this is only possible because of the grace we are afforded in Christ.

Amidst my own frailties, this principle is one that I purposefully practice, though with great pain at times. My reasoning is simple: I know the amount of stupid things I have done. I know how unworthy I am of God's grace. I know I've said and done awful things out of the messes of my own experience. And I know how many times I have been forgiven, by others and, more importantly, by God. It's a sobering thought.

Forgiving Yourself

Publius Syrus said, "How unhappy is he who cannot forgive himself." I've always believed that the majority of us are much too hard on ourselves. We all make stupid mistakes and dumb decisions. We hurt people unintentionally or even intentionally; we say things we don't mean that have lasting effects; we act before we think; and the list goes on and on. And even if we experience the gift of forgiveness from others and from God himself, many of us are plagued by those awful memories.

A good friend of mine, who suffered from several addictions for over fifteen years, felt she had squandered a good portion of her life. One area of concern was her finances. Ironically, she had a fabulous career in finance and, in my estimation, was brilliant and wise beyond her years. (I think she still is.) For a long period of time, however, she was obsessed with knowing things she wasn't supposed to know. For a number of reasons, she found herself paralyzed by fear of things out of her control, specifically concerning relationships, and sought answers from self-proclaimed psychics. It became an addiction that cost her roughly twenty thousand dollars within a year and a half.

She became fixated on how a certain young man felt about her. When she couldn't get a straight answer from him, she panicked and phoned psychics, some of whom charged twenty dollars a minute. On several occasions she contacted up to thirty psychics a night to assuage her fears, give her direction, and basically make her feel better. At one point her eyes opened to the absurdity of her addiction. She deleted her online accounts and even technologically banned herself from being able to access the websites. It didn't last very long.

Toward the tail end of her experience, she soberly realized the reality of her dwindling bank account. Shame quickly overwhelmed her initial numb feelings, and she spent days sleeping off the truth of what she was doing and what she had done. One day she recognized that she couldn't do it anymore. Through spiritual meditation and study, she realized she had to let go of the obsession, not only for the sake of her finances but also for the sake of her sanity and her health. The most excruciating act in surrendering her addiction was having to forgive herself for spending twenty thousand bucks on people who had used her vulnerability to their financial advantage. She told me, "I literally had to hug myself. Imagine how hard it is to hug yourself and say, 'Honey, you did the best you could. I know you screwed up royally, but it's okay. You are going to make it through.' Imagine how difficult it was to forgive myself when all I could think about was that I was a fat, disgusting failure doomed to a life of solitude and pain." It broke my heart to hear her say this to me.

She shared how she was finally able to let go of her own grievances because she couldn't be realistically and healthily connected to God if she couldn't make peace with her mistakes. And then she said something quite powerful: "When I look back at that period, I can still feel the pain I was in, so I just try not to think about it because I forgave myself, God has forgiven me, and that pain is part of the past. It has shaped me for the ultimate better. The experience hasn't disappeared from my memory, but it doesn't haunt me anymore. We have to somehow find ways to forgive ourselves, change our ways, and vow to make better decisions so that history doesn't repeat itself and we create a better chance for ourselves to live happier lives."

This reminds me of one of Jesus's disciples, Peter, who was quick to speak and frequently found himself with his foot stuck in his mouth. He was loyal, that's for sure; he stuck by his Master's side like glue and on many occasions, with a loud bellow, proclaimed his faithfulness to Jesus. Mark records that at the Last Supper, Jesus turned to Peter and said, "Satan has asked to sift each of you like wheat. But I have pleaded in prayer for you, Simon Peter, that your faith should not fail. So when you have repented and turned to me again, strengthen your brothers" (Luke 22:31–32 NLT). This is something that nobody wants to hear. Can you imagine hearing from God, "The devil wants to have his way with you, and I told him okay. But don't worry. I'm praying that in the end, you'll be okay." How's that for causing someone to feel visibly uncomfortable or, more likely, appalled? Our response would probably be, "What? Are you nuts? Tell the devil to leave me alone! Isn't that your job?"

But Peter didn't budge. His response was typical: "Lord, I am ready to go to prison with you, and even to die with you" (Luke 22:33 NLT). The Gospel of Matthew states that in that same conversation, Jesus told all of his disciples that they would betray him, to which Peter piped up and said, "Even if everyone else deserts you, I will never desert you" (Matt. 26:33 NLT). Peter doesn't seem fazed by the possibility of playing pawn to the evil one's schemes. He probably thought there was no way on earth that he would ever disappoint his Savior. "After all," Peter probably imagined, "I'm different. I'm not like those other followers of Christ. I will not let Jesus down."

I'm sure Jesus must have sighed with compassion before he uttered a prophecy that seemed unreal to his bold, warrior-like confidant: "Peter, let me tell you something. Before the rooster crows tomorrow morning, you will deny three times that you even know me" (see Matt. 26:34). In other words, "As I'm on the way to the cross, where I'll hang like a torn piece of butchered meat, you won't be around to save me. You won't be there to help me out. You won't be there to advocate my cause. As a matter of fact, you will deny you ever knew me. And you'll use a few choice words to make that point clear. You will make the case that you were never in relationship with me."

Stubborn Peter was still adamant about his loyalty and insisted, "Even if I have to die with you, I will never deny you!" (Matt. 26:35 NLT). Hours later, as Jesus stood in the courtyard of the high priest with the crowd demanding his blood and shouting his guilt, Peter watched from a distance. In the middle of the chaos, a young woman turned her face toward Peter's direction and recognized him as being part of Jesus's crew. She called him out on it. "Hey you, over there, I know you. You are one of them, with the Galilean Jesus guy." The first denial escaped his lips as he feigned innocence. "I don't know what you're talking about" (Matt. 26:70 NLT).

Minutes passed and another random soul approached Peter with the same question. This woman made it her mission to garner attention from the folks around her, and she told everyone who would listen that Peter knew Jesus. A second time Peter snapped and retorted that he didn't know the man who was about to be pummeled by Roman guards. Still later, after curiosity got the better part of the crowd, another person came up to Peter and said something like, "Wait a minute. I know you keep saying you don't know this guy Jesus, but I can tell from your accent that you're lying. You must be one of the disciples." This time Peter let loose and swore, "A curse on me if I'm lying—I don't know the man!" (Matt. 26:74 NLT). And at that exact moment, in the distance wailed the predicted crow of a lone rooster, unaware that his shrill cry did more than welcome the crack of dawn; it shattered two hearts. The Bible is vividly poignant in its description of Peter's reaction—"Suddenly, Jesus' words flashed through Peter's mind. . . . And he went away, weeping bitterly" (Matt. 26:75 NLT).

Peter staggered away from the courtyard away from the Messiah he had just claimed he didn't know, away from his Teacher, who was moments away from getting the beating of his life. All of Peter's vehement promises to protect and pledge allegiance to Christ exploded into meaningless fragments. At the very least, Peter was crushed. It's one thing to feel incredibly dumb after saying something stupid. It is another thing to break a vow made only a short time before leaving the scene of the crucifixion of the one to whom you made the vow. Peter wept bitter tears, and I'll bet he had a tough time forgiving himself for his actions. Chances are he never did until his encounter with Jesus after the resurrection. We don't know where Peter was while the cry of "My God, my God, why have you forsaken me?" (Matt. 27:46) leapt out of Jesus's swollen and bloody lips. We don't know exactly what Peter was thinking. But we can assume he was mentally and emotionally beating himself up.

When three women followers of Jesus went to the tomb on Sunday, they were greeted by an angel and told, "Don't be alarmed. . . . You are looking for Jesus the Nazarene, who was crucified. He has risen! He is not here. See the place where they laid him. But go, tell his disciples *and Peter*, 'He is going ahead of you into Galilee. There you will see him, just as he told you'" (Mark 16:6–7, emphasis added). "Go tell his disciples," was the message, but something was missing. It was more like an intentional pause. "And tell Peter," they added. "Relay these words specifically to the guy who is probably kicking himself in the pants right now, unable to forgive himself for what Jesus already knew would happen. Tell Peter the good news. Tell Peter that Jesus is going to be paying him a visit. And tell Peter it's going to be a good one."

It's difficult and may seem impossible to forgive yourself after betraying the God you have committed your life to, but our literal saving grace is that he already knows how we will mess up. We don't surprise him by our failings. And while we are wallowing in self-defeat, self-pity, and the mire we have crawled, stepped, or jumped in, Jesus makes an individual intervention on our behalf. He says, "I will tell the world my Good News"—and he inserts our names in here—"I will tell it to Jimmy and to Brenda and to Paul and to Steven and to Nicole and to you." Peter needed to know Jesus forgave him, for that was the only way he would be able to step out into the calling that he was destined for. And it was the only way that Peter was able to forgive himself.

Aftershocks

Forgiving someone or being forgiven doesn't remove the natural or intentional effect of consequences. I think about the forgiveness we are offered by God—the grace we are afforded when we repent of the wrongs we have committed—and how he responds by saying, "I forgive you. I remember it no more. Now go in my peace." While that grace exists in all its wonderful power, sometimes we have to deal with the repercussions that follow our wrongs. A man who is guilty of adultery can be forgiven by God but might have to endure an ensuing divorce. A woman who murders another can be extended grace from God but will probably have to sit in jail for the rest of her life. And if we have hurt someone on whatever level, we may have to stomach a disconnect in that relationship, even after experiencing forgiveness from that person and from God.

One of my best friends has endured tremendous pains caused by me for different reasons. We have had a friendship going on eight years now, and she is one of my closest confidants. She knows everything about me; there are no hidden secrets between us. But I'll be honest: in my addiction stage particularly, I lashed out at her many times and said some pretty mean things to her. One time I even distanced myself from her on purpose without giving her any reason for my actions. I disappeared like a phantom, which made me look like I more than took our friendship for granted. When we were roommates, I bailed out of my lease and stuck her with a new roommate whom we soon found out had a bunch of personal problems and turned out to be a bad roommate.

Through these situations and others, she has forgiven me many times. I am quick to point out that it was totally my fault. But our relationship took frequent beatings as a result of my actions. Still, in spite of our relational lapses and struggles, she continually forgave me. She taught me an incredible lesson in the area of forgiveness, and I give her a lot of credit for developing that part of my own character.

Forgiveness may not be an easy place to work from, but it is what we are called to do. And whether we have caused offenses or have been on the receiving end of them, it is something we have to practice through—and many times *only* through—the grace of God. To you, my dear readers, who have experienced unthinkable infractions or injustices—my heart goes out to you. I cannot dictate how to find the space of grace in your heart to forgive, but I can only say that finding that area is the only way healing can begin. It is the only way that wholeness can be restored. It is the only way that God is able to take even the most evil ordeals in our lives and somehow, in his own mysterious and miraculous way, weave in peace and ultimate good. May we learn to forgive others, learn to forgive ourselves, and through it all be reminded of the many instances he has extended that same favor to us in our own messes.

8

THE DEMONS OF ADDICTION

An addict is someone who uses their body to tell society that something is wrong.

Stella Adler

I was in love once. With a man who was probably an alcoholic. I think he was, but he was the functional kind. You would never have even guessed it had you not realized that he liked to drink a lot. In our conversations the word *alcoholic* was never mentioned, though *drink too much* was. But other people who knew him mentioned the "A" word. It's not for me to judge him or, heaven forbid, label him as one yet it was clear he had some kind of drinking problem. The addicted seem to have a keen ability to sniff out addiction in others. We notice the signs because we are so adept at hiding, lying, running, evading, pretending, and so on ourselves. This was why I knew some sort of mess was at hand.

I had known him since I was a teenager. He was a tough guy on the outside; half tough, half marshmallow on the inside. He always said what was on his mind, though his language at times was colorful and usually absent of filters. I, for one, appreciated his candor; I'm sure he offended plenty others. All gruff manner and behavior aside, he was very charming. Funny. He oozed confidence through every pore. He loved his mother. He was handsome. He was, as I had once referred to him, "my perfect." Oh, how the flair for the dramatic emerges in the midst of utter stupidity.

At different points in my life I had even thought I was going to marry him. Most of those times I was in my "God told me" phase. During one of those phases God was telling many couples in our church to tie the knot, and I wanted to be part of that club. I can't say God told the guy anything, of course, but I hoped and prayed that God would start forcing him to look at me as wife material.

I should tell you that our relationship status never officially rose above the friendship level. I should also tell you that he had been dating a girl since the second grade, or sixth grade, or something as crazy as that. Just seeing these two sentences on paper makes me cringe. I guess it assures my status as a former love-smitten nut case.

We definitely had an intimate, almost inexplicable connection, one that he would even admit to years later. We got each other. We were safe zones for one another. But the reality of what happened, with such consistency it should have violently exorcised the fool out of me, was inescapable. We would be incredibly close friends for a while; then he would drop off the face of the earth. After a few months or even a year or two had passed, we would reconnect and resume our incredible closeness. And yes, then he would disappear again.

This cycle recurred so many times that any reasonably healthy person would get the picture and start backing off for good. Not me. At the time I didn't think the inconsistency was indicative of our friendship being unstable, unhealthy, or anything negative. I believed it meant the forces of evil were exhausting themselves trying to keep us apart. Clearly, in my immature and warped mind, we were meant for each other, at least at some point down the road.

The emotional seesaw was pointless, though, as he ended up getting married to the girl he had been dating since forever. I found out about it a year and a half after they sealed the deal. I'd tell you I was heartbroken. Shattered. Crushed. But it was worse. When I randomly saw their wedding picture in a friend's home (that's how I found out they had gotten hitched), I felt like Chucky had lurched out of the frame of the happy couple, plunged a hatchet into my chest, and started hacking me into bite-size pieces.

A few years later they got divorced. Can you guess what came next? Yup, we united in epic fashion. He said things to me that I had longed for him to tell me for years. All that I-love-you-I-always-loved-you-I-have-been-thinking-about-you-all-this-time-I-don't-know-what-happened-before-yada-yada-mushy-gushy stuff. And I unknowingly tumbled backward into the emotional tunnel of hell while I resounded my praises toward heaven because God had finally brought "the one" back into my life. I knew it! I just knew it was true all along.

So he and I got reacquainted. We resumed our special whatchamacallit. We rekindled a friendship that was something more than platonic but still never rose to a romantic level. A few months later he disappeared. He has not contacted me since. Through the rumor mill, I heard a wide variety of gossip as to what had happened to him. Someone told me it was drugs. Others said that he was drinking himself to death. Or that he was having an affair with a married woman. Or that he had gotten back with his ex-wife. Or that he had post-traumatic stress disorder and had snapped in a nervous breakdown fashion. It didn't matter. He had hurt me to the point of utter devastation. And Chucky lurched in my direction with a deadly twinkle in his eye.

I should have known better. That much is true. I chose to ignore some obvious signs. During our latest reconnection phase, he informed me that he had no feelings. He was an emotional wasteland. I had sent him a really nasty email (in my own drunken stupor) in which I basically told him I hated him. He commented that while he felt bad when he read it, he wasn't fazed. His emotive capacity was, at best, the size of a petri dish. But I attributed it to the various traumatic events he had experienced and made myself believe that he really did have strong feelings for me. I was quite an impressive liar.

On several occasions we had three-hour-plus conversations where we were vulnerable and honest with each other, our dialogue peppered with mushy gushy "I've always loved you" stuff. And every time he called me the next day and asked, "Hey, did we talk last night? I don't remember anything." One time, out of sheer frustration, I asked him what his intentions were with me. His response? "I don't even know what my intentions are with my own life."

Let me be clear that I can only give you my perspective on the situation. I still don't know what happened to him, except that a good friend of mine who recently spoke to him said he had gone to rehab. Apparently during his journey toward sobriety, he had reached out to a bunch of people to apologize for his past behavior and such. I, of course, wasn't on this list. In an effort to uncover some truth, I recently sent him a two-line email, to which he responded without once asking how I was, where I was, or what I was doing or even saying something along the lines of "I'm sorry."

To be honest, it was embarrassing. Not so much for him as for me. I was shamed by having been through whatever it was I went through with him and him not acknowledging what had happened. I had been blinded by a lie. I had been eclipsed by something I wanted so desperately that I took whatever crumbs I got and tried to make it into a five-tier wedding cake. The truth was that the friendship I had unduly exalted was really one part imagination, one part need, one part fribble. All parts lies.

I can look back and see the traces of addiction, particularly because my own demons were clawing at my eyes during some of our reconnection phases. Deep down inside, I heard the lies coming a million miles away. I knew how addicts become a shell of person. How, in feeding our addiction, we say and do things that are almost not of our selves. We are liars, and we are good at what we do. This man lied to me on several levels, but more importantly, I lied to myself. I imagined an intimacy that just wasn't there, and so I naively made excuses for his erratic and hurtful behavior.

Recently I watched the award-winning movie *Leaving Las Vegas* with Nicholas Cage and Elizabeth Shue. It's a great movie even though it shows the ugly reality of addiction in a make-you-want-to-hang-yourself sort of way. A career alcoholic (played by Cage) living in California is fired from his job because of his drinking problem. His addiction is so bad that he has given up even trying to hide it. After he gets canned, he empties his checking account, dumps the contents of his home into an orderly array of black plastic garbage bags, hops in his car, and drives to Las Vegas, bottle in hand. His plan is sick yet simple. He will stay in Sin City and drink for however long it takes to kill him. With remarkable accuracy, he estimates it at only a few weeks.

In Vegas he meets a stunning hooker (Elizabeth Shue) who houses her own personal demons, and after a night of sharing nothing more erotic than talking and spooning, she falls in love with him. Eventually she asks him to move out of the sleazy hotel where he is staying and move in with her, though she is fully aware of his suicide mission. He balks at the seemingly crazy request, but then agrees. He tells her, "You can never, never ask me to stop drinking. Do you understand?" Fighting back tears, she responds, "I do. I really do." And for a few weeks they are not quite lovers but a pair of hurt, angry, and codependent souls who share an emotional affair of unhealthy proportions.

Watching this movie was quite painful for me on many different levels. What struck me most, however, was that neither of them really lied about their destructive realities. There was no need. He knew she turned tricks at night. She knew he would die with shaky fingers gripped tight around a half-empty bottle of poison. Yet many addicts aren't as truthful about their particular situations. They wreak havoc on their lives and others' because they can't help it. It's who they are. They lie about the fact that they have an addiction. They lie about their true feelings, which most times they wouldn't even be able to recognize anyway. They lie about the severity of their dependency. Pains are ignored. Fears are disregarded. Insanity is camouflaged.

The truth of who they are is too painful and embarrassing to feel, to admit, to experience, to grapple with. So numbing is the only option. If they have not even the slightest desire to get help, not even God himself can help, though he is more than able to. "The truth will set you free," the Bible says (John 8:32). Truth himself is able to bring to light dark realities. The beauty of his truth covers the ugliness of our truth. That is the hope for the Christian addict . . . if we want it bad enough. That, of course, is the kicker.

The Christian and the Addict

I have often wondered about the relationship between the Christian and the addict. I think most of us would rather pretend such an affair wasn't possible. Wouldn't it be great if once we became followers of Christ, we were given protective gear for addictive tendencies and compulsions? Wouldn't it be nice if our urges to excessively indulge in something harmful could be stopped dead in their tracks by a BB gun pellet with a Jesus imprint? Maybe it would be better if we wore Holy Ghost jumpsuits that reflected anti-addiction, radioactive beams to prevent these desires from coming within even two feet of our holiness. No such luck. Now, I understand that not everyone suffers from an addiction or even addictive tendencies. Plenty of people are naturally self-controlled and disciplined in pretty much all areas. But plenty of others are struggling.

I want to focus on the faith-based addict. Some people come to Christ with monkeys on their backs, and others find themselves addicted to something in the course of their spiritual walk. No matter how they got there, Christian addicts exist. The Barna Group reports that one out of every eight Christians deals with an addiction that personally haunts them. So what's our poison? The study wasn't specific, but I know what you're thinking. Alcohol. Drugs. Porn. Food. Those are the things that we normally associate with addiction, aren't they? I'm sure there is someone that we know who is addicted to something. The ones about whom we can say things like: *He loves his liquor more than his wife. She smokes pot like it's going out of style. He's on the computer all night, and he's not checking the weather. She never eats, and when she does, she goes to the bathroom for some odd reason and runs the water.*

No Christian would do these things, right? Heaven forbid. We see each other on Sundays or at our small group meetings and present ourselves as well-dressed folk who carry Bibles, share sunny smiles, give good hugs, and wave adieu with our manicured hands as we leave in shiny cars. Nobody wants to associate addiction with Christians. It doesn't mesh well. And it's embarrassing. If Christians can't get it right, for goodness' sake, what hope is there for the rest of the world? How are we Christians supposed to go door-to-door, hand out tracts with cartoon drawings of demons and hell, and convince people to "turn or burn"? What sort of pathetic example are we? What happened that we woke up one morning lacking immunity to repulsive habits and numbing behavior? What is wrong with us?

Then there are the more blurry addictions. The ones that we probably do a better job at hiding. The ones that, if we're not careful enough, or paying close attention to, or really seeking truth, can destroy us equally as much as an obsession with liquor, painkillers, or sex. Ever think about being addicted to religion? It's not a new concept and has been talked about quite frequently in different circles. You go to church so much but for all the wrong reasons. You don't want to get spiritually fed or relationally connected; you just want to feel a sense of moral superiority. You feel more comfortable following black-and-white rules than having to "work out your salvation" (Phil. 2:12) in a personal way. Christians who don't meet your rigid expectations make you uncomfortable, and you add them to your prayer list under the "backsliders" section.

Basically, religious addiction is when you look, walk, talk, sound, and act like a Pharisee. In John 9 Jesus heals a beggar who was blind at birth by giving him a weird set of instructions. Jesus spits on the ground, mixes his saliva with mud, slaps it over the eyes of this guy, and tells him to wash in a pool called Siloam. Jesus

THE DEMONS OF ADDICTION

is looking, sounding, and acting like a kook right about now, but worse than that, he's also committing a religious snafu. Apparently, at that time, keeping the Sabbath holy meant you couldn't heal anybody on that day. But the blind man stands by Jesus, holy spit and dark earth smeared over his good-for-nothing eyes, and he does what Jesus tells him to do. As he plunges his body into the murky waters and leaps out, he is dripping wet, smelling of algae, and grinning from ear to ear. He opens his newfound eyes and sees colors and objects and people and things that he can't even associate with words yet because he's never ever seen them before. I mean, really, the guy never even knew what mud looked like. Or water. Or a human being.

When his neighbors find out what happened, they bring the beggar before the Pharisees, who, rather than feeling an incredible sense of awe and wonder, feel troubled and end up accusing the man of lying about getting healed by Jesus. Some of them remark, "This man Jesus is not from God, for he is working on the Sabbath," and "But how could an ordinary sinner do such miraculous signs?" (John 9:16 NLT). This poor man starts feeling like a circus freak on what is likely the best day of his life. The Pharisees are so outraged, they call his parents to find out whether or not he was really blind to begin with. Then they continue to harass the man, asking him to repeat his story over and over. What was their problem? Jesus didn't fit in their religious box. He didn't follow the rules. And instead of being open to the mystery of the divine, they freaked out and were bothered by something they could not explain and something that they even considered "unlawful." This wasn't an isolated incident. The Pharisees often did things like this.

You can be addicted to religion in the worst sense. You can be more obsessed with following the commandments than with loving God and others. You can be more concerned with preaching to show off your oratorical skills than with feeding your sheep. You can be involved in every program, committee, or special event at your church and become more and more like a ghost at home to your spouse and kids.

I don't know if you are struggling with something, if you are recovering from something, or if you even care about this topic. I just want to say that addictions are a problem, even for Christians. We are not immune. While lately the church has done such a better job of creating recovery programs and other support groups for those who need help, we need to individually be more aware of these issues and deal with them appropriately.

Instead of looking at the symptoms—which is what they are anyway—of drinking, smoking, sexing, and drugging, we need to be more spiritually sensitive to the source of the acting and lashing out. It's not enough to put down the drink or stop hopping into bed with anything with a skirt. A ton of arduous internal work must be done. For most addicts recovery is not an instantaneous experience. Perhaps this is the biggest challenge for a Christian addict.

In the Absence of a Microwave Miracle

At some point on the addiction journey of our lives, we often start to view God as a cure-all God. A spiritual Santa Claus. A magician who can pull cuddly rabbits out of hats and shiny coins from our ears. On one hand, this is not necessarily a bad thing. I'm not talking about superficially comparing God to David Copperfield; I'm talking about believing that God is able to do the impossible. As it concerns the addict and recovery, this means praying and believing that we get delivered, sooner rather than later, from the monkeys on our backs. Let's be honest: pulling an elephant out of a yarmulke seems more doable.

Yet how can we not pray for this? How can we not ask for his intervention? We would be fools not to. The book of James offers, "You don't have what you want because you don't ask God for it" (James 4:2 NLT). If prayers work . . . if there are legitimate realities to faith and believing . . . if we are taught to ask anything of him and it shall come to pass, then why not believe him for anything and everything? Why not ask for our addictions to instantaneously disappear? Why not ask for him to cut us free from the noose around our necks?

Certainly we have all heard testimonies about such supernatural stories. "I woke up one morning and I lost all of my urges to smoke, drink, snort, or shoot up. I've been sober ever since." It is encouraging, exciting, and even hopeful to sit back and hear someone advertise such immediate deliverance. What greater proof is there that something, or more specifically Someone, exists outside of and is greater than even our most disciplined selves?

While these are nothing short of miracles, they are still rare occurrences. Let me tell you, there are more people sitting in AA meetings, seeing therapists, being supported by much-needed sponsors, and having to live "one day (or hour) at a time" than there are Christians who stand in church services giving praise reports about their addictive urges going AWOL. If you think that every Christian is supposed to experience Johnny-on-the-spot liberation, you are wrong. Just ask the believer who spends every Sunday at the altar begging to have her addiction vanish. Just ask the people who sit in Al-Anon meetings week after week and fervently pray for their wife or their sister to just stop drinking. Just ask the parents of the twenty-five-year-old woman who weighs sixty pounds and will die unless she starts eating or continues to be fed intravenously for the rest of her life. Just ask the cocaine addict who comes to the altar every Sunday with recurring dreams of acting out one of the final scenes in the movie *Scarface* where Tony Montana snorts a Mount Everest of blow up his nose before he is killed.

It can be frustrating to begin the journey of recovery with your only arsenal being the flickering knowledge that you have a problem and a blind trust in God to help. The process of getting better is backbreaking. At times it feels impossible. Other times it makes you feel so ashamed. So you start to put pressure on God to make your addiction immediately go away. Oh, the overwhelming despair of believing in a God who has parted a sea, initiated powerful conversions, and cured diseases yet waking up each morning with your addiction staring back at you with its beady eyes. Many times we think something is wrong with us. That we are not working hard enough, or don't want recovery bad enough, or don't have enough faith. Such lies keep us from the beauty of trusting him day by day, inch by inch.

If our addictions don't disappear, we pray to make the process less painful. Easier. One where not as many tears are required. Where not as much work is needed. Where not as much self-evaluation is necessary. But maybe we should be changing, or rewording, our prayers. Maybe instead of begging for a microwave miracle, we should be begging for God's presence. Begging for his strength, his grace, his peace. Begging for him.

I don't doubt that God can make your addiction go away in a millisecond. I don't doubt that he can make the journey as easy as a light jog in Central Park. I don't doubt that recovery can come quickly. But I also know the deep measure of trust in him that we must possess. That if we cannot have our magical remedy, we must solely cling to him, believing and hoping in his promise that "those who trust in the LORD will find new strength. They will soar high on wings like eagles. They will run and not grow weary. They will walk and not faint" (Isa. 40:31 NLT).

The three most popular prayers associated with Alcoholics Anonymous are the Serenity Prayer, widely credited to theologian Reinhold Niebuhr; the Lord's Prayer, found in the New Testament; and the Prayer of Saint Francis, widely attributed to a thirteenth-century saint named Francis of Assisi.

The Serenity Prayer

God grant me the serenity
to accept the things I cannot change;
courage to change the things I can;
and wisdom to know the difference.

The Lord's Prayer

Our Father which art in heaven,
Hallowed be thy name.
Thy kingdom come,
Thy will be done in earth, as it is in heaven.
Give us this day our daily bread.
And forgive us our debts, as we forgive our debtors.
And lead us not into temptation, but deliver us from evil:
For thine is the kingdom, and the power, and the glory, for
ever. Amen.

Matthew 6:9–13 KJV

The Prayer of St. Francis

Lord, make me a channel of thy peace;
that where there is hatred, I may bring love;
that where there is wrong, I may bring the spirit of
forgiveness;
that where there is discord, I may bring harmony;

that where there is error, I may bring truth;
that where there is doubt, I may bring faith;
that where there is despair, I may bring hope;
that where there are shadows, I may bring light;
that where there is sadness, I may bring joy.

Lord, grant that I may seek rather to comfort than to be
    comforted;
to understand, than to be understood;
to love, than to be loved.
For it is by self-forgetting that one finds.
It is by forgiving that one is forgiven.
It is by dying that one awakens to eternal life.

Notice the depth of these words: "Accepting things we cannot change." "Give us our *daily* bread." "Lead us not into temptation." "Make me a channel of peace." You cannot do these things without being in continual communion with God. It requires constant prayer for peace to rest in his presence; for grace to make it through another twenty-four hours with sobriety and in abstinence; for help in surrendering to his will; for the power to die to self and live with an eternal purpose. And it requires thanking him for the miracle of still being alive.

Relying on God day after day, hour by hour doesn't sound as exciting or make as good a story as being instantaneously delivered does, but it makes for such a spiritually amazing experience. It is a passageway into seeing the scope of God's faithfulness mysteriously and beautifully unravel on a daily basis. Yes, this can happen even in the middle of the hard work we have to do; the shame that tags along with seeing how we have abused our minds and our bodies and neglected others; the relapses or slipups that may come; the embarrassing times when we have to ask others for forgiveness;

and even the times when fragments of an addiction that we think we have fully recovered from appear out of nowhere.

Picking Up the Pieces

I was angry. I was venomous. My emotions were like bitter poison, and it penetrated every syllable and every breath when I said, "Well, it's your fault. You were the one who got mad when I asked you if I was pretty."

I said this to my mother in what I thought was a flippant manner. I acted nonchalant when really I was violently flinging my emotional garbage—the crap I had long ago thrown in a duffel bag and shoved under my bed—at her face because at the time I didn't want to deal with the real issue. I had just eaten too much at Thanksgiving dinner and felt like a pathetic, bloated glutton from the pits of hell.

During this holiday a few years ago, my mom and my sister-in-law were chatting like old friends on the living room couch. They were talking about parenting skills and having husbands. Things which I knew nothing about. I was probably angry because of that too. Here I was, an attractive, intelligent woman with no husband, no kids, and no potential in any of those directions. And here was my beautiful sister-in-law, three years my junior, with two utterly dynamic kids and a perfect husband under her belt. And a glamorous career. And a beautiful home. And she was thin, and I had eaten three rolls with butter.

So I spewed poison. That's what happens sometimes with people who are recovering from or even have overcome addictions. Because we no longer can take the comfortable avenue of dealing with or numbing whatever is bothering us, the nasty feelings sit there inside of us. If we're not careful and if we're not paying effective attention, they fester. They become irritated. And they grow. Like fungus. George Carlin said it like this: "Just 'cause you got the monkey off your back doesn't mean the circus has left town."

When we let our feelings smolder, they usually come out in words or emotions that are ugly and hurtful—like accusing my mother, in front of people, for being my bulimic catalyst. It wasn't her I was angry with; it was me I hated. She had nothing to do with anything but just happened to be in the wrong place at the wrong time, talking about things that I wanted to be a part of and that I had always dreamed of having. I didn't know how to appropriately shush my jealousy or even address it, so the self-loathing started to seep through my pores. And my mind welcomed it because it was comfortable.

I sat at the kitchen table, half mindless, half self-loathing. All of a sudden my brain organized an elaborate pity party in my spirit and the guest of honor, self-loathing, took over. I began to indulge in wicked mental gluttony. I hated the fact that I was almost thirty and single. Almost thirty and paraplegically climbing my career ladder. Almost thirty and still lugging around a roll of fat around my middle. Almost thirty and disgusting. That was what I was telling myself.

The self-awareness of former addicts needs to be significantly higher than the average person's. That's because we've spent years recklessly yielding ourselves to bad behavior and self-deprecating thoughts. We've never thought of challenging our mind or habits. We've lived like zombies, drunk from our addictions, numb to reason, and unconscious of sanity. If a random thought tells us we're good for nothing, then by golly, it must be true. If we think we're lazy, or incompetent, or a bad father, or a miserable boss, then surely it is reality. We know no different. We listen to the pieces of our conversations that feed us self-hatred. And we agree, because at the time we know no better and have not galvanized any defenses against it. We are our thoughts. And we are ugly human beings.

On the road to recovery, you are taught to create toolboxes—crates filled with emotional, mental, and spiritual resources to combat yourself, the you that is destructive. You are taught to maintain abstinence or sobriety by using the equipment accordingly. The beginning, of course, is usually the hardest. If I overate, for instance, I didn't have the option of throwing up; I had to instead quickly find healthy self-dialogue. I calmly asked myself why I ate so much and what I was feeling at the time and then coaxed myself away from the demons that were begging me to stick my finger down my throat. I had to repeat phrases in my head: "It's okay, you didn't eat that much." "Throwing up will only take you miles back in your recovery." "You are beautiful."

I don't have the intense addictive urges today that used to plague me. But what I do have are the remnants, the little pieces, of the bigger issues. The stuff that made me want to engage in destructive habits to begin with—the insecurity of who I am inside and out, the desire for people to like me, and even sometimes the daunting whisper that I am still not good enough as a Christian or as a girlfriend or as a daughter.

In these moments, absent of the option to mask my feelings or even isolate myself from everyone else, including God, I remind myself of the verse, "The truth will set you free" (John 8:32 NLT). I don't use psychological jargon to appease whatever it is I am feeling. I'm sure it works for some people, but not so much for me. What I do is pray. Pray like crazy. Pray like a mad woman on crack. I purge my feelings in an honest and sometimes an even seemingly irreverent sort of way, and I rely on God to cover my truth with his truth. I remind myself of my worth in him that is so eloquently woven throughout Psalm 139:

> I praise you because I am fearfully and wonderfully made;
> your works are wonderful,
> I know that full well.
> My frame was not hidden from you
> when I was made in the secret place.
> When I was woven together in the depths of the earth,
> your eyes saw my unformed body.
> All the days ordained for me
> were written in your book
> before one of them came to be.
> How precious to me are your thoughts, O God!
> How vast is the sum of them!
> Were I to count them,
> they would outnumber the grains of sand.
> When I awake,
> I am still with you.

vv. 14–18

I cling to Jesus with reckless abandon because in those moments I have decided that he must be enough. Just Jesus. Nothing and nobody else. Just him.

Addiction—The Modern-Day Golden Calf

I recently read a fantastic book called *Addiction and Grace* by Dr. Gerald May, in which he explores the relationship between addiction and spiritual awareness. I was intrigued by his comparison of modern-day addiction with idolatry. May writes,

I am not being flippant when I say that all of us suffer from addiction. Nor am I reducing the meaning of addiction. I mean in all truth that the psychological, neurological, and spiritual dynamics of full-fledged addiction are actively at work within every human being. The same processes that are responsible for addiction to alcohol and narcotics are also responsible for addiction to ideas, work, relationships, power, moods, fantasies, and an endless variety of other things.

We are all addicts in every sense of the word. Moreover, our addictions are our own worst enemies. They enslave us with chains that are of our own making and yet that, paradoxically, are virtually beyond our control. Addiction also makes idolaters of us all, because it forces us to worship these objects of attachment, thereby preventing us from truly, freely loving God and one another. . . .

Spiritually, addiction is a deep-seated form of idolatry. The objects of our addictions become our false gods. These are what we worship, what we attend to, where we give our time and energy, instead of love. Addiction, then, displaces and supplants God's love as the source and object of our deepest true desire. It is, as one modern spiritual writer has called it, a "counterfeit of religious presence."[1]

After Moses miraculously leads millions of Israelites out of Egyptian slavery, as told in the book of Exodus, the event planning committee hardly has any time to coordinate a victory party. With fresh wounds, bruises, and scars on their formerly shackled ankles and wrists, the Israelites tearfully watch as more trouble approaches. This nation has to contend with a succession of events and saboteurs that test their fortitude and, most importantly, their desire to trust in the God who had led them out of bondage in the first place. Round one launches with the Egyptian army on their tails. Then comes round two, the grumbling of a million hungry bellies and hoarse whispers from parched throats. In round three they are ambushed by the Amalekite army, whom they somehow vanquish in another miraculous episode.

At this point, about three months into their forty-year journey, they enter the Desert of Sinai, a place they will stay for about a year. They set up camp, and almost immediately Moses makes his first of three treks to the top of a mountain to hear the message God wants to tell the nation of Israel.

There the Lord directs Moses to keep the memories of their exodus alive. The Israelites are to remember the Lord's past faithfulness, to remind themselves how he has never abandoned them. In doing so, they are to serve no god or idol or person, place, or thing other than God. Some time after Moses comes down and delivers the communiqué, God decides to literally show up in the camps and reveal a fragment of his physical presence.

After a series of intricate preparatory events, God manifests himself to them in a dramatic and mind-blowing display of power and might. He's covered in a fierce silhouette of billowing smoke and blazing fire accompanied by the sound of the trembling mountain and the blare of majestic trumpets. After this electrifying scene, God tells Moses to come up the mountain so he may lay down some housekeeping rules. Among the litany of regulations God gives Moses are the Ten Commandments.

As Moses is basking in his mountaintop experience with God—overwhelmed, I'm sure, by the vast amount of responsibility he is given in leading these people and now having to help them follow these pretty lofty standards—the people of Israel start to get antsy. They are itching all over. From what? Boredom? Nervous anxiety? Stress? They start to doubt whether or not Moses is ever coming down. "When the people saw how long it was taking Moses to come back down the mountain, they gathered around Aaron. 'Come on,' they said, 'make us some gods who can lead us. We don't know what happened to this fellow Moses, who brought us here from the land of Egypt'" (Exod. 32:1 NLT).

Moses is taking forever. But really, in their estimation, it is God who is taking too long, and they are tired of waiting around. They think they have better things to do. So they bully the guy who is second in command into making them an idol out of jewelry so that they can worship it in their leader's absence. You realize, of course, how ridiculous this sounds. Only a short while earlier, their eyes and ears were fixed on the shrouded presence of God. It was unmistakable. He was a breath away. And now, frustrated, discouraged, and desperate for a quickie feel-good kind of something, they throw their gold hoops, silver bangles, and shiny ankle bracelets at Aaron's feet and tell him they will bow down to whatever he happens to craft from a pile of their bling.

Long story short, it doesn't even seem like Aaron takes any time to think this through. Matter of fact, as the story is told in the Bible, apparently Aaron doesn't even blink his eyes before he says, "Sure," and gets started on the job. "Then Aaron took the gold, melted it down, and molded it into the shape of a calf. When the people saw it, they exclaimed, 'O Israel, these are the gods who brought you out of the land of Egypt!' Aaron saw how excited the people were, so he built an altar in front of the calf. Then he announced, 'Tomorrow will be a festival to the Lord!'" (Exod. 32:4–5 NLT). Except, of course, it wasn't a festival to *the Lord*; it was a festival to *a golden calf*. A baby cow made of gold.

The next day they party themselves silly. The Israelites run amok, are out of control, and so "become a laughingstock to their enemies" (Exod. 32:25). They cause such an embarrassing amount of commotion that even God can't stand it any longer. Fuming, he orders Moses to get down from the mountain and straighten his crooked people out. Moses does so with impassioned fury.

"We want an idol and we want it now," the Israelites demand. "We want something we can touch and see and smell and taste. It's the only way to take away these unbearable pressures and pains and fears that torture us because you, God, are not here." Isn't this common vernacular from the addict? Isn't this sentiment a huge part of what an addiction is?

"This life is too much for us," we cry. "So I need to drink, drug, sex, cut, work, and spend because it makes the hurt disappear . . . at least for a little while." A little while of something is better than a long while of nothing. In these moments we feel like God is simply not enough. This is what we say when we habitually indulge in things that are outside of him. This is what we say when we make golden calves out of our jobs, our spouses, our prestige, our money, our position, our power, our drugs . . . you name it.

God, you are not enough.

One of the reasons I am grateful for having gone through an addiction is the front-row ticket I got into recognizing all the different ways I was telling God that he wasn't enough for me. The greatest part of recovery was being able to come before him alone in dealing with my myriad fears, insecurities, hurts, pains, and shattered dreams.

Addiction is definitely a form of idolatry. It keeps us from the One who is love. It holds us back from experiencing a complete relationship with the very source of being. It prevents us from experiencing full-fledged spirituality, that which is only able to be birthed through the ultimate surrender of our will and the letting go of whatever lucky charms we are clenching in our closed fists.

What are you addicted to? What are you holding on to so tightly because it feels better than trying to grasp at God's invisible hand through wisps of air? What do you use as a crutch instead of relying on God as your ultimate source for everything? What do you use to cope with life instead of kneeling down at the feet of peace himself? Whom do you bow down to instead of worshiping the Maker who wove us in the epitome of perfection?

I'll bet so many of you keep your idols in a choke hold because letting go leaves space for a question that you are too frightened to even ask, let alone explore: "Is God even enough?" In the darkest holes of our addiction, we don't bother asking because we don't need God. We have whatever we use to numb or anesthetize or forget. But once stripped of those defenses and left naked and exposed, we realize that the only thing we really have in this world is God. And if he is all we really have, *is* he enough?

9

IS GOD ENOUGH?

God is the universal substance in existing things. He comprises
all things. He is the fountain of all being. In Him exists everything
that is.

Lucius Annaeus Seneca

I believe the true measure of the depth of spirituality comes in
times of crisis. When we are sucker punched by disturbing realities.
When we lose everything we thought was important to us. When
we are left alone with burning questions that will sometimes remain
unanswered. It is in these moments that we find ourselves haunted
by the question, "Is God enough?" Is he enough in my life to deal
with the loss of a loved one? Is he enough to deal with the shame
of shoving executed bankruptcy documents in our file cabinets?
Is he enough to deal with a cancer that is slowly eating away at

our insides? Is he enough to deal with overcoming addictions that once served as the only sure thing we had in our lives?

The challenge of being a believer is in serving a God who—however full of goodness, grace, mercy, and peace—has parts that do not sit well with us in times of distress. He is part mystery, part unknowable, and, at times, seemingly absent. He is also invisible. I believe we see glimpses of him through creation and even through people, but let's be honest. We can't physically touch him. Most of us don't audibly hear him. We can't pick up the telephone in the midst of our catastrophe and listen to him give us an inspiring and encouraging pep talk about why things are turning out the way they are, or how tomorrow things will definitely be different in a good way, or how in three months the prayers we have desperately prayed will be answered.

Yes, we have the Bible we can rely on. I recognize that, and I am grateful for it. But sometimes, for me at least, I feel that it is not enough. I want concrete answers and suggestions and commentaries, and I want them now. I also know that I am not alone in this frantic quest. This is why so many people struggle with addictions, are codependent in relationships, and work so hard to become self-sufficient. Some people even abandon the whole God idea altogether. They cannot rest in mystery or unknowing, so they cling to whatever it is they cling to, whether ideologies or people or stuff. Because at least those things they can see, feel, and touch, whereas trusting in God in a world so full of disappointments, struggles, trials, and traumas seems more enigmatic than anything else. Or even foolish. But while doing this may provide us with comfort or confidence in the interim, quite frankly, it is dangerous.

Sometimes in periods of utter tragedy, we are left with these two options: have faith in spite of God's intangibility and invisibility, or gratify our anxieties in ways outside of God himself. Because he is not meeting our needs or turning life out the way we imagined, many of us are tempted to focus our attention on numbing our disappointment. We can drink ourselves into oblivion to make the pain manageable for a couple of hours. We can indulge in the love given to us by the spouse who has pledged eternal allegiance to us. We can rest in hefty bank accounts. We can rely on whatever our innate gifts, talents, and abilities provide us with.

The question "Is God enough?" becomes too much to bear, so without even beginning to wrestle with the question, we shut him out. God tells us in his Word, "Here I am! I stand at the door and knock. If anyone hears my voice and opens the door, I will come in and eat with him, and he with me" (Rev. 3:20). *The Message* puts it this way: "Look at me. I stand at the door. I knock. If you hear me call and open the door, I'll come right in and sit down to supper with you." Is God there? Absolutely. He is knocking, he is ringing our doorbell, and he is looking through our living room window. But sometimes we are nowhere to be found. We are working more late hours at the office. We are getting stoned in the backyard. We are hiding under our bedcovers, afraid of facing life. We are doing laundry, pretending that life is okay and we are just fine. So we don't hear the knock. We don't hear the doorbell. And we certainly cannot see him peering through the windows of our souls.

One of the greatest things we can do in our faith walk is to understand that our confidence is found in him and him alone, because, as most of us would agree, life happens. Stuff happens. People die. Natural disasters occur. Pink slips come. Good health fails. People betray us. And if we cannot rest in his presence, whether or not we feel it, we will remain lost and will internally suffer and become embittered by life's inevitable injustices.

Who Is Your Source?

In times of trouble, confusion, or uncertainty, we seek counsel from our friends, from wise mentors, from counselors, from on-line quizzes, from self-help books, and even, in the case of one of my friends, from psychics. Doing some of these things may be fine. But at a certain point we begin to overextend our reliance on things or people when we should instead be pointing our troubles, confusion, and uncertainty toward God. I know why we do it. We do it to feel better—to somehow unravel the knots in our stomachs that make us toss and turn all night and prevent us from focusing on what we need to focus on.

But who is God to us if he cannot be enough? I believe he is our source—our source for life, for breath, for emotional health, for physical sustenance, for financial resources, for love, for peace, for everything. This is easiest to believe when life is running a smooth course and we have made it so we are pretty competent in satisfying our particular needs and wants. This is hardest to believe when those resources crumble. When the spouse we have relied on for the past twenty years walks out the door of a supposed eternal commitment. Or when we are fired from the cushy job we had. Or when our demons of addiction, the ones who have left us alone for a time, start to claw at our backs. It is really in those moments that we are forced to admit in what secret place our deepest sense of security is found.

I am not saying we should not have some level of dependence on people or things, but it would serve us well to recognize that these are mere channels through which God operates and that even if we were depleted of those things, God alone would be sufficient. But, oh, what a tough concept that is to live out in the absence of resources that are real, tangible, and evident.

In my case, for instance, every time I found myself in an unbearable situation, I was inclined to call ten different people and talk out my problem with them. Good people, mind you, not random strangers I met on the street. But instead of being left with peace, I was left with more anxiety. I was looking for definite direction. I wanted a quick fix. I longed for a word or two that would eradicate my problem, and it was easier to hear audible remarks, however wise or foolish, than to have faith in the still, small voice.

Why didn't I just go to God? Sometimes because I felt he was absent. And sometimes because I didn't want to hear what he was going to say. And sometimes because I didn't think I could tell the difference between what he was saying and what my subconscious was saying. Sometimes I felt more comfort (though temporary) in hearing my wise brother offer advice. This was not necessarily a bad thing to do, but honestly, it got to the point where I wasn't doing what I should have been doing, which was coming to God first as my ultimate source. I know many people who rely on their spouses for unconditional love, approval, security, stability, and a whole slew of other things. I suppose if you repeat the vows "for better or for worse," you are somewhat entitled to get some of those things. But surely there must be a problem if God is left out of the equation.

Who is your source? Who or what do you rely on first when you start to hit bumps on the highway of life? I'm sure many of you have been in situations where you have needed to hold on to faith for dear life, when you felt stuck in a concrete room without windows and doors and had no choice but to either rely on the Unknown to get you out or to close your eyes, wither up like a prune, and waste away in misery. If we are to live out our faith walk, the whole faith thing must come into play. Yes, sometimes it can feel like a gut-wrenching process. Believe me, I know. But it's also powerful and can shape your spiritual journey in life-changing ways.

A King in the Wilderness

In the Bible we are first introduced to David when he is a young shepherd boy. A relative nobody. A kid even his family was quick to overlook. Most of us are familiar with his subsequent victory over the Philistine giant Goliath using a sling and a single stone. A boy who tended sheep and was the youngest of his family kills an enemy—one whom some historians peg at standing over nine feet tall—in less than a minute. Clearly God was behind the match. Through the prophet Samuel, God anoints the boy as the future king of Israel, though this is not made a public spectacle. His royal destiny is kept private.

After Goliath's defeat, the people of this nation sing their praises to David. Even King Saul is impressed, but only for a little while. David rises in rank and catches the eyes of all around him. He becomes more than a bold boy who killed a giant; he is skilled in many areas. He is a great musician, possesses remarkable leadership ability, is a fearless warrior, and is even a wise politician. King Saul eventually sees this young man as a formidable threat and starts to squirm uncomfortably in his royal robes. The green-eyed monster bites King Saul where it hurts most—his pride—and his jealousy starts to overtake his soul. He puts a contract on David's life, and this shepherd boy, whose forehead is still shiny from the anointing oil, begins a several-year run for his life, evading a king who intends to kill him. His story is told in 1 Samuel. His flight begins in chapter 20 with the words, "Then David fled" (1 Sam. 20:1).

You can imagine David's bemoaning. One day he is a nobody; another day he is told by a prophet that he has been chosen to be the next king of Israel. And a good while later, he embarks on a long, tiresome run to save his hide. He is not a king by any stretch; he is a fugitive. David's heart must have sunk to an immeasurable depth. Perhaps he even wondered if this whole king thing was a sham and he would spend the rest of his days looking behind his shoulder.

How many times has the same thing occurred in our lives? We pursue dreams, missions, and objectives and tirelessly devote much of our time, energies, and emotions to them, only to watch as they fall apart or crumble right before our eyes. The disappointment sets in, and God seems to be a phantom watching from a distance. Do we throw up our hands in surrender, callously swallow our bitter pill, and find something other than God to assuage our letdown? Or does a better instinct nudge us to cement ourselves in God and trust in him that even though things seem dismal, simply holding on to him will be enough to get us through?

Could God have been saying something like this to David? "I have destined you for great things. I have made plans for your life that rest beyond even your wildest dreams. But before they actualize and you sit on the throne with a golden crown adorning your head and hold the incredible power of ruling a kingdom, you are going to spend time in the wilderness. You are going to go to a place of great desolation where you will wonder if I am even there . . . if the dreams I have designed for your future are really true . . . if the victory of killing a giant and defeating a mighty army even mattered. You will walk through the valley of the shadow of death, abandoned even by the people who love you. You will be alone, hungry, tired, beaten, worn, distracted, afraid, longing, depressed, and devastated in spirit, but you will see that I am enough. You will discover that your trust isn't found in chariots or armor or good looks or your prestigious title. You will eventually see and feel, with vivid clarity, that your true confidence is found in me, the one who formed you in the womb and has called you out by name."

David learned to trust in God. While the Psalms, many of which were authored by David, clearly illustrate his depression and anxiety, his measure of faith in the Lord is just as apparent. Read these passages of Scripture that David wrote while running from a murderer and note the duality in them:

Psalm 13

How long, O LORD? Will you forget me forever?
　　How long will you hide your face from me?
How long must I wrestle with my thoughts
　　and every day have sorrow in my heart?
　　How long will my enemy triumph over me?
Look on me and answer, O LORD my God.
　　Give light to my eyes, or I will sleep in death;
my enemy will say, "I have overcome him,"
　　and my foes will rejoice when I fall.
But I trust in your unfailing love;
　　my heart rejoices in your salvation.
I will sing to the LORD,
　　for he has been good to me.

Psalm 56

Be merciful to me, O God, for men hotly pursue me;
　　all day long they press their attack.
My slanderers pursue me all day long;
　　many are attacking me in their pride.
When I am afraid,
　　I will trust in you.

In God, whose word I praise,
    in God I trust; I will not be afraid.
    What can mortal man do to me?
All day long they twist my words;
    they are always plotting to harm me.
They conspire, they lurk,
    they watch my steps,
    eager to take my life.
On no account let them escape;
    in your anger, O God, bring down the nations.
Record my lament;
    list my tears on your scroll—
    are they not in your record?
Then my enemies will turn back
    when I call for help.
    By this I will know that God is for me.
In God, whose word I praise,
    in the LORD, whose word I praise—
in God I trust; I will not be afraid.
    What can man do to me?
I am under vows to you, O God;
    I will present my thank offerings to you.
For you have delivered me from death
    and my feet from stumbling,
    that I may walk before God
    in the light of life.

King David wasn't a perfect man by any means. His life was messy. Even when he was officially ordained as king over Israel, problems never left him. He had a whole set of other issues he had to contend with and wrote more of the Psalms during that period. But what never waned was his honest trust in God. He frequently repeated prayers like this one: "God, my situation sucks.

Everyone is on my case. Nothing seems to be going right—not even the things that I believe you have called me to do. I hurt. I am pained. I am afraid. But I will trust in you. I will continue to put my confidence in your hands." David penned the most famous psalm, one that many of us have had memorized, at least partially, since we were kids:

Psalm 23

The Lord is my shepherd, I shall not be in want.
He makes me lie down in green pastures,
he leads me beside quiet waters,
    he restores my soul.
He guides me in paths of righteousness
    for his name's sake.
Even though I walk through the valley of the shadow of
    death,
I will fear no evil,
    for you are with me;
your rod and your staff,
    they comfort me.
You prepare a table before me
    in the presence of my enemies.
You anoint my head with oil;
    my cup overflows.
Surely goodness and love will follow me
    all the days of my life,
and I will dwell in the house of the Lord
    forever.

See, David learned that though life was wrought with twists, turns, and heartache, his best bet would be to rely on God. David realized through his wilderness experience that God had to be enough. God was enough without the glitz and the glamour, without the immediate answers to prayer, without the instantaneous miracles—and God was enough even in the presence of betrayal, moral crisis, and a broken family life.

I believe that God is really enough if we let him be. He's enough if we are aware of his presence, if we latch on to his right hand, if we trust in the midst of our blindness, if we roll in the mud with uncertainty. This is not an easy task. Some of us want to simply disappear when life pins us against a wall with its grimy hands. Others of us would rather spend our time looking for escape hatches outside of his presence. "But blessed are those who trust in the LORD," the Bible tells us, "and have made the LORD their hope and confidence. They are like trees planted along a riverbank, with roots that reach deep into the water. Such trees are not bothered by the heat or worried by long months of drought. Their leaves stay green, and they go right on producing delicious fruit" (Jer. 17:7–8 NLT). Blessed are we when instead of looking outside of him to make ourselves feel better, we look to him.

The Problem of Walking on Crutches

A danger can be found in relying on God with defensive motives: it's basically fake. It's like using a pair of feeble crutches when we don't really need them. I know this is one thing that I have struggled with. I have a deep fear of abandonment. Though I have worked on this with different therapists and have put much effort and prayer into abolishing this fear, it occasionally creeps up. This comes from having experienced relational disappointments where people have literally disappeared, intentionally or otherwise, out of my life.

The first happened when my father died when I was fourteen years old. I was the poster child of a "daddy's girl." He was the only adult who I could rely on for unconditional love. He loved me regardless of my behavior, my attitudes, my idiosyncrasies, and what I looked like. One evening he went to bed with a headache and asked me to pray for him in what I believe was a desperate attempt to fight with God for his life and to say good-bye to his little girl. He never woke up. An aortic aneurysm exploded in his heart, and as the blood rushed through his body and his stomach bloated up in a grotesque, disfiguring shape, my sister traumatically tried to bring him back to life. It didn't work. He was here that morning and gone that night.

I had resolved, or so I thought, the issues of dealing with the death of a parent until I reached young adulthood. But then people started mysteriously dropping out of my life. This happened on so many occasions that my sister and my best friend, Doyline, frequently talked about how odd it was. It wasn't normal, I guess. As a result, I unconsciously developed a tough interior that I placated with my heartwarming nature. This hardened throughout the years.

Since I was in my early twenties, I desperately wanted two things: to spend the rest of my life with a man I truly loved and to become an author. I believed God had put these desires in my heart. After a series of dispiriting happenings that made me feel like these desires would never be fulfilled, I became overwhelmed with severe anxiety. The anxiety eventually turned to anger and bitterness. I was having quiet time one morning when in my spirit I heard a question: "A. J., if these things never came to pass, what would you do?" I almost broke into a cold sweat, and I hissed back, "What? Are you kidding me?"

But almost instantaneously I was overcome by an indescribable calm, in which I could hear the question posed again and I had the wherewithal to really think about it in a rational way. "If these two 'dreams' never came true," I wondered, "what *would* I do?" My response was simple. I would be upset, depressed, frustrated . . . and then it hit me. Really, what would I do? Retire my zeal for life? Become an atheist? Be overcome with bitterness? Kill myself? It was at that moment I realized that, sure, I'd be disappointed, but my life wouldn't be over. Time would continue to tick and tock, and I would have no choice, really, but to function as healthily as I could, pick up the shattered pieces of my heartbreak, trust that God is working out other things in my life, and move on. I realized then that God must be enough. His love for me, as it concerned his will and purpose for my life, must be enough. Relying on his mysterious ways must be enough.

This is what has carried me through the many pains and let-downs that have come my way. But I'll be honest: there were times when I shut down, on all levels, with people because I was so afraid that I would be abandoned by them. I also tried hard not to expect anything, even any good gifts that God might send my way. I justified my defensiveness with the understanding that God was all I needed. I was somewhat callous in my thought process that I should do my best not to rely on anything or anyone for whatever I thought I needed. And clearly, this wasn't the right thing to do. Honestly, I still need my heart softened sometimes. If I need something from a person or if my soul desires something, I tend to squash the reality of my want and protectively say, "Well, who cares. I don't need anything; I just need God. Whatever. Big deal." But apparently it is a big deal to me. And God cares.

I am learning to trust that he is enough, that he ultimately knows what he's doing, and that I don't have to be such a hardhead through the journey. We face a grave temptation to become bitter when people or circumstances fail us. This is where we use God more as a crutch than a source. We do this to protect ourselves, just in case. Really, however, it robs us of a certain joy that is found when we accept that he is on our side and when we trust, as Paul wrote, that he will meet all of our needs (see Phil. 4:19). Listen, we do need people and stuff in our lives. We need friends we can count on. We need to have purpose and direction. We need money to survive. But we must understand that God is still good enough, regardless of what we have.

Is God enough? He is. But I also know this question is one that must be meditated on regularly. And it is not one that should be answered based on our feelings or our circumstances. The messiness of faith allows for us to balk at the question sometimes. To admit that there are some days when we're not entirely sure. Yet if we truly claim to be followers of Christ, then the core of our heart must be rooted in his sufficiency for all things. Big things and little things. This type of assurance only comes through communion with him. In *The Ragamuffin Gospel*, Brennan Manning writes, "In essence, there is only one thing God asks of us—that we be men and women of prayer, people who live close to God, people for whom God is everything and for whom God is enough. That is the root of peace."[1] May we learn through traveling in our faith how to live with confidence in God, resting in his everlasting arms, and may we mirror the sentiment behind the psalmist's words, "My flesh and my heart may fail, but God is the strength of my heart and my portion forever" (Ps. 73:26).

10

THE TREASURES OF DARKNESS

My wings are folded o'er mine ears,
My wings are crossed o'er mine eyes,
Yet through their silver shade appears,
And through their lulling plumes arise,
A Shape, a throng of sounds.

Percy Bysshe Shelley,
Prometheus Unbound

Darkness is bad. Just ask any child who has forged a dependence on a night-light. Just ask anyone walking through an unlit alley at two in the morning. Just ask a widow who lies awake under a moonless sky, desperate for dawn to break. Just ask a lone hiker lost in the woods on an autumn night.

But there is another type of darkness, the internal kind that shadows our souls at different times and for different reasons through circumstances that sucker punch our otherwise satisfactory existence. These are things like the hulk of depression that can sink its teeth deep into our lives with no reasonable explanation; the sudden death of a loved one; the experience of a debilitating disease that wastes away our bodies and our minds; the painful scabs of an addiction, a bankruptcy, a devastating mistake, an unanticipated failure.

Darkness is void of even a glimpse of light. It is a place that seems absent of hope, of possibility, and of opportunity. Darkness can be bleak, dismal, and depressing. It's a frustrating space to live in, especially when in the midst of your darkness, the world around you continues to spin on its axis. Life moves on, even when you feel like time has stopped for you. People all around you celebrate births, marriages, anniversaries, holidays. And in your own world, bills still need to be paid, the dog still needs to be fed, dinner still needs to be made. Life goes on in full circle.

I'm sure plenty of you have even experienced what many spiritual traditions call "the dark night of the soul"—a broad sense of a crisis of faith. This is where God seems absent. The foundation of a naive, childhood Sunday school faith or even a mature, tried, tested, and true faith starts to shake. Questions that you might have never dreamed of asking seep through the surface of your being. Does God care? Does he know what he is doing to me? Is my faith a sick joke? Is God even real?

I knew a young woman who I believe may have been obsessed with Mother Teresa. She even spent time working with the Missionaries of Charity organization in Calcutta. To me it seemed that this woman glorified Mother Teresa's faith as being consistently and irrefutably solid, without question or doubt. And this woman I was acquainted with emulated the same type of faith she believed her icon experienced. It was like she lived in an ethereal place every hour of every day, a 24-7 ecstasy of sorts. Her world was like a pink bubble filled with butterflies, puppies, rainbows, and daisies. The dark realities of life were melted by her seemingly drug-induced, sappy smile. God forbid her joy could ever be crushed by a blow, or even a mild tap, of doubt.

When recently the world became a witness to the internal spiritual struggle of the late Mother Teresa through her spiritual directors, I thought about what a shock it must have been to this young woman. The beloved nun had revealed her dark night of the soul, a night that lasted roughly fifty years. She was an incredible woman who had sacrificed the bulk of her life to serving the poor, sick, orphaned, and dying in India. She was recognized throughout the world for her charitable efforts and was admired by millions of people as a living example of Jesus himself. But during the later part of her incredible journey, Mother Teresa was tormented. In her diary she painfully wrote, "In my soul, I feel just the terrible pain of loss, of God not wanting me, of God not being God, of God not really existing."[1] It was a wake-up call to the spiritual community, but not in the sense of discrediting faith or pointing mocking fingers at a religious figure who struggled with belief. It simply sobered many of us to the truth of the union of the imperfect path of faith and the necessity to keep on moving and believing anyway.

My own life has been cluttered in darkness, sometimes for stupid reasons and sometimes for legitimate ones. I have been around the block a few times in wrestling with my faith, oft times writing about it and hoping that light existed somewhere out there beyond the dark. At times I felt abandoned by God. At times I felt I had so grossly wasted my life that hope had run out on me. At times I felt that I had somehow missed what God was trying to say to me and so he had given up on me. My journal entries reflected this sentiment. Here is one of them:

I think God has forgotten me. Like he offered me a multitude of chances I didn't take. Chances that I was either too blind to see or purposefully avoided for whatever reason. I missed my boat, as they say. I didn't even know I had to book my ticket, to be honest, and now I'm stuck. Then why won't he kill me, I wonder? Why? It doesn't make sense. If I don't get "IT," then surely I'm a lost cause, and why focus attention, love, answered prayers, and hope on a human being who is a reject? Why not throw away the bad milk? I don't know. I haven't figured it out yet. Do I want to die? A part says yes and the other no. Equal parts.

I look at the others. The perfect people. The admirable Christians. Beautiful, smart, respected, quiet, kind, disciplined. And then I look at me. The bulimic. The broken wheel. The cursed promise. The shadow of sadness. I am marked by addiction. Scorned with a monkey on my back that would give King Kong a run for his money.

What happened to me? Where is the promise? Why did my strong faith disappear? When did the "you just never know" positive attitude fall to the wayside? Where did I fail? Where did I fail? Many times. Many times over and over. My life is the Ferris wheel I wrote about when I was twenty. It keeps going around and around and around. No one is telling me how to get off. I try to climb off, but I get stuck on the metal spokes. I try to jump off, but the belt loop on my jeans gets stuck on the seat. I try to scream to get the attendant's attention, but he is too busy smoking a cigarette and staring at giggly, sixteen-year-old hotties. So I try to enjoy my ride, and at times I do. But the fiftieth time around I get nauseous and try to yell, jump, and crawl off again. And no one is listening and helping me off this stupid circle.

Is my only choice to believe that this is it? Am I supposed to just do my best and keep enjoying this never-ending ride that is making me sick? Is this my lot for my fervent prayers? My fighter attitude? My pursuit of faith and belief? My demand for change, redemption, healing, and rescue? I honestly feel all of these things go unheard. They have fallen on deaf ears. I have been refused by the One who created me and was supposed to be my eternal refuge. He is in another camp with better people than I, and I am on the Ferris wheel. Still. How sad for me. How sad.

On one hand, this makes me want to cry and hug myself. On the other hand, it makes me happy because I know ultimately God was there. I wasn't alone, I wasn't a cursed promise.

Treasures in Darkness

In the book of Isaiah, a prophecy was written about King Cyrus, the first king of Persia, about two hundred years before he was even born. At the time of the fulfilling of these prophetic words, the Jewish people were held captive by King Nebuchadnezzar of Babylon, a city known at that time as the capital of the world. For seventy years they found themselves once again enslaved under tyrannical rule. Their beloved temple had been destroyed, the wealth of their nation had been pillaged, and the familiar weight of shackles mercilessly bound them.

But after seventy years, the time had come for God to liberate them. It was time for the nation of Israel to be delivered by sovereign hands. And God did this in the most unusual way. He stirred the heart of King Cyrus, an influential ruler who had no meaningful ties to the Israelites. This leader was quickly creating a reputable name for himself and was widely known specifically for his benevolent nature. Throughout history he has been hailed by such names as Cyrus the Enlightened Liberator, Cyrus the Law-Giver, Cyrus the Righteous, Cyrus the Heroic Conqueror, and many others. Isaiah tells of God's commission to King Cyrus and how he was chosen to deliver the Jewish nation from the bondage they were in. Isaiah 45 opens up with this passage:

> This is what the LORD says to his anointed,
>   to Cyrus, whose right hand I take hold of
> to subdue nations before him
>   and to strip kings of their armor,
> to open doors before him
>   so that gates will not be shut:
> I will go before you
>   and will level the mountains;
> I will break down gates of bronze
>   and cut through bars of iron.
> I will give you the treasures of darkness,
>   riches stored in secret places,
> so that you may know that I am the LORD,
>   the God of Israel, who summons you by name.
>
> Isaiah 45:1–3

And in perhaps one of the easiest conquests in history, King Cyrus and his troops marched into the city of Babylon and conquered a people who took pride in being better on so many levels than everyone else. The royal leaders of the city were in the middle of a great party when they found themselves invaded by their enemy. Babylon's mighty warriors were drunk, as were the guards who had, in the middle of their blitzed stupor, forgotten to bolt shut the iron gates of the city. Babylon didn't know what hit them as the Persian army literally walked through the front doors of their kingdom. Forming even the slightest resistance was impossible.

So the great city of Babylon fell, and King Cyrus set out to do what the Lord had tasked him to do. He not only released the Israelites from captivity but also gave them back what King Nebuchadnezzar had stolen from them years ago. The Persian king encouraged them to rebuild the temple that had been destroyed prior to their enslavement. He motivated them to restore what they had lost and even equipped them financially by commanding the Babylonians to give the Jewish people silver, gold, livestock, and supplies. Not only did the Israelites gain their freedom but they were given treasures, gifts from their enemies to aid their cause and provide restitution so they could fulfill their divine purpose. God didn't just want their chains to break; he wanted something to be rebuilt in the process.

It's a great story that speaks of God's continued faithfulness, his plan for restoration, and his willingness to use whoever needs to be used to get something done. When I read Isaiah 45 for the first time, my heart was stuck on the words "treasures of darkness" (v. 3). I didn't know the context of the verse, and I didn't interpret the message as finding treasures in a literal or a materialistic sense, but those words spoke to me.

I thought about the dark places we trudge through. I thought about my own dark places and wondered about my own treasures. I took a trip down memory lane, slowly beginning to connect some of the dots of my story—the valleys of addiction and depression, the mountaintops of recovery and hope, and everything else in between. There was a tie, though for the most part it was not obvious to me back then.

Darkness can be so overwhelming that sometimes it is almost impossible to gain even a vague sense of clarity. Everything is blurry. Shadows dominate the spaces that are hungry for life. Our souls ache in anguish. We are depleted of our resources and find ourselves emptied of everything except, if we so choose, a blind trust in God. And as our throats get raspy from the constant repetition of the same prayers, we find him sitting beside us. The frustrating part is that we can't see him. Sometimes we are lucky enough to feel his presence. We miraculously sense a nudge of the divine, the slight assurance that he has never left and he never will.

Looking back, not only was God's presence evident throughout each step of that part of my messy journey of faith, but there were treasures of darkness to be found. Not silver or gold but things even richer. Peace was birthed in the most volatile of places. Strength appeared when my physical body had no energy except to lay in bed. People were placed in my life by God to offer me grace, joy, laughter, and love. I even received divine revelation, a silent comfort that somehow everything was going to be fine. A healing process was straightening my crooked places. Prayers received answers that can only be attributed to miraculous intervention from God himself. I felt the instilling of the truth that all was not lost, that he would step in and show up. That he would take whatever I had managed to make or even salvage of my life and, with his gentle hands of mercy and a gracious providence, would gladly receive my ashes and return them as beauty.

If there is one thing that I have learned and that has been a prominent theme in my life, it is that none of us walk out of darkness empty-handed. Restoration exists. Healing is available. Rebuilding can come. Not only that, but sometimes the darkness is a mysterious treasure itself. It is through these times that the depth of our faith is authenticated. All of the ideologies we have pledged allegiance to are tested. Is what we believe about God and about ourselves really true? Do we really love him as much as we say we do? Is the Christian faith really worth it? Does believing in him matter at all? Do we trust him enough, even through the unknown?

If you find yourself sitting in the middle of darkness, you are usually quickly thrown into the process of wrestling with these thoughts. And if you keep holding on, if you keep believing, if you don't let go of the truth that he has not left and that he really cares, the words "God will never leave you nor forsake you" (see Heb. 13:5) will carry such an intense meaning that they will change your life and deepen your faith. This is the treasure of darkness. In the middle of broken spirits, shattered fragments of failings, and the life tragedies that knock us off our feet, and when we have lost all sense of self-sufficiency, God sweeps into our broken places in the most gentle of ways. And with a fragrant sweetness, he shapes our messes, saturates them with his Spirit, and wraps them with purpose.

Nothing is impossible for God. Nothing is beyond his intervention. Nothing is greater than his deliverance. "I will go before you," God says. "This is where you understand this is not about you but about me. You simply need to be quiet, stand still, and let me take care of this on my own. I will go before you. I will level your mountain of trial. I will break down the bronze gates of your desperate situation. I will cut through the iron bars of your mess."

In my life I have been faced with mountains, stopped in my tracks by gates of bronze, and frustrated by bars of iron. Nothing in my own inner strength or intellect could have paved a way through those obstacles. Nothing in me could have conquered the darkness that hid my treasures. There comes a time when we need to stop trying so hard. Not that we give up on or stop doing the right things, but we must surrender our man-made plans and stop trying to find a way out of things on our own. We need to stop playing God. We need to put down our game strategies and life manuals and let him do the work. Why? So that we may know that he is the Lord, the God who summons us by name. So that we may know that we can walk in triumph through the darkness and the valleys of the shadow of death if we are holding on to his hand. Minnie Louise Haskins wrote a poem which beautifully illustrates this point:

> And I said to the man who stood at the gate, "Give me a
>   light, that I may tread safely into the unknown,"
> and he replied, "Go out into darkness and put your hand
>   into the hand of God. That shall be to you better than
>   light and safer than a known way."
> So I went forth, and finding the hand of God, trod gladly
>   into the night. And He led me toward the hills, and the
>   breaking of the day.

A Secret Surprise

Anxiety is something I struggle with. Maybe I shouldn't, for a slew of reasons you or I could give, but the fact is, I do. Sometimes it's a pest, and other times it is outright overwhelming. I remember one day when I had hit the unbearable wall of writer's block; as I reread my ninth draft of a chapter in this book, I became miserable. The amount of time, energy, and emotion I was pouring into writing *Messy Faith* seemed pointless. My words looked like a colossal string of meaningless consonants and vowels smashed together in an overflowing kitchen garbage bag. I wondered if I even had it in me to finish the book. In an effort to distract myself, I went to a local spa to get a facial.

The ride to the spa was full of frustration. I was mad at God for creating a person who had to deal with a constant noose of depression and fear. I was mad at him for giving me a task

I was clearly too incompetent to complete. I was mad at him that I could not exercise the "joy of the Lord" (rolling my eyes) I witnessed so many of my peers experiencing. I was mad at him because I was disappointed in myself. As I plopped myself on the plush couch in the spa waiting room, burning with a smorgasbord of emotions, I was greeted by my facialist—a tiny woman who looked to be no more than eighty pounds soaking wet. Ringlet curls framed her petite face, and as she introduced herself to me, I noticed her Minnie Mouse voice matched her appearance perfectly.

For the next sixty minutes, something mysterious happened. Normally in moments of anxiety, I get very quiet. The last thing I want to do is talk. Especially to someone who I don't know anything about except for a first name. But something about her lightened my mood. After we exchanged introductions and small talk, our conversation took a peculiar turn. She admitted to me her struggle with depression. She shared how she wanted to go back to church. She talked about her marital struggles. And then she told me that that day was supposed to be her day off, but for some reason she felt a pull to go to work, even though she was having one of her mentally and emotionally bad days . . . or maybe because of it.

Our dialogue centered around God, of course, and I was able to share with her my own experiences of mental torment and the faith I had in God to pull me through. Yes, even though I had seethed on the way to the spa and thrown a tantrum before his holy presence. This lady appreciated my honesty. Tears filled her eyes, and she told me she believed that I was the reason she was supposed to go to work that day. I was a blessing to her, she said, because I offered a smidgen of hope . . . of faith . . . of a God who is love . . . of a God who has never left her and who beckons her home. To say the least, I was flooded by humility and felt an inch tall, because in talking to her, I had experienced a similar kind of hope.

And in that dark place of mine, in that crevasse of uncertainty and frustration, while I was clouded with anger and disbelief, I was nudged by the Eternal. God surprised me. I was given a treasure—the reminder that we have brothers and sisters all around the world and that we all need each other. I was reminded that we are given chance human encounters to exchange not just meaningless conversations but words of hope and encouragement. I was reminded that we can walk through the doors of some place feeling discouraged and walk out of the same place, even just minutes later, with a smile on our faces.

We must pay attention to these secret riches, these divine surprises. In a weird kind of way, every one of us is a unique treasure to other people. Sometimes we don't even realize this, because we think our treasures should come in the shape of something big and dramatic, like the parting of a sea or the conquering of a city. But treasures of darkness can come through people, through our caring for them, through our loving them, through our making an intentional difference.

A Light in the Dark

In 1880 in the small town of Tuscumbia, Alabama, Helen Keller was born a normal baby girl. Her physical body was perfect. Her entire being was in working order. There was nothing wrong with her, and her parents, like most others, were delighted in this newborn bundle of joy. When she was nineteen months old, however, she came down with what doctors diagnosed as an "acute congestion of the stomach and the brain." The illness, though temporary, left her deaf, blind, and mute.

Helen transformed from a normal baby girl into, in her own words, something "half-human, half-animal." She endured the next five years of her life in this miserable state, void of effective communication and having to rely on disturbing and disruptive ways of getting whatever she wanted. "I know I was impelled like an animal to seek food and warmth. . . . I was like an unconscious clod of earth. There was nothing in me except the instinct to eat and drink and sleep. My days were a blank without past, present, or future, without hope or anticipation, without interest or joy."[2]

It didn't take much for her to be provoked into raging tantrums. She kicked. She grunted. She bit. She hit. She pushed. Her parents, distraught by the situation, were unsure of what to do, so they allowed Helen to act in this animalistic manner. They enabled her to live in perhaps the lowest level of human functioning. They reasoned that she didn't know any better and, sadly, would probably never know any better. I'm sure they did the best they knew how.

Helen's behavior got so bad, though, that her parents decided as a last resort to enlist the help of a teacher called Anne Sullivan. Anne, who had been blind at one point in her own life, came to the house and began to teach Helen how to properly communicate. Using a special language of spelling words on Helen's hand, Anne tried to show her that words existed for things. Everything had a name. But this wasn't something Helen easily understood. She was able to imitate her teacher's actions, sure, but she connected no meaning with it. The whole process seemed pointless. Needless to say, Helen was a terrible student. She even locked her teacher in a room to abort this learning process that, in the little girl's mind, was something closer to torture than help. But something shifted one day.

With great frustration, Anne had been spelling w-a-t-e-r in Helen's grubby hands over and over again. Helen became angrier with every calculated movement of Anne's finger, and Annie in turn became more discouraged. Finally Anne grabbed the disabled girl, forced her outside of the house, and put her in front of a water pump. Annie furiously pumped the cool, gushing water into Helen's palm and repeatedly spelled out w-a-t-e-r with the other hand. W-a-t-e-r. W-a-t-e-r. W-a-t-e-r. She repeated this over and over and over. Finally it clicked.

Helen described the event as an awakening of her soul. "All at once there was a strange stir within me—a misty consciousness, a sense of something remembered. It was as if I had come back to life after being dead. . . . I wanted to learn the name of every object I touched. . . . Nothingness was blotted out. . . . That first revelation was worth all those years I had spent in dark, soundless imprisonment. . . . The world to which I awoke was still mysterious; but there was hope and love and God in it, and nothing else mattered."[3]

Helen was never the same after that and eventually became a champion for the deaf and the blind. She found secret riches out of her disability, her literal darkness. She was a voracious reader, an avid believer in and pursuer of education. She learned, she wrote, she taught, she campaigned. She created for herself a legend that has never diminished in influence.

I don't know how dark your night is. I just know that your dark places are not pointless. They are not devoid of God's hand of providence. You will not enter back into the light without a sense of purpose, without a life-changing conversion experience, without a refined spirit, and without a greater confidence in God.

Light will penetrate all of the spaces of our lives either by tiny cracks or open plains or something in the middle. Isaiah writes,

Arise, shine, for your light has come,
　　and the glory of the LORD rises upon you.
See, darkness covers the earth
　　and thick darkness is over the peoples,
　　but the LORD rises upon you
　　and his glory appears over you. . . .
The sun will no more be your light by day,
　　nor will the brightness of the moon shine on you,
　　for the LORD will be your everlasting light,
　　and your God will be your glory.
Your sun will never set again,
　　and your moon will wane no more;
　　the LORD will be your everlasting light,
　　and your days of sorrow will end.

Isaiah 60:1–2, 19–20

I don't know how messy your faith is. I just know that God is there. I have no eloquent words to help you on your journey other than to tell you he is right beside you. He longs for you. He wants you. He has not given up on you. He has not forgotten about you. And no matter what the picture of your unique road of trusting in God looks like, know that he is right there. His presence is unchanging and eternal.

Faith is not just messy. It is not only an experience of struggle, despair, and hard times. So much beauty and joy and peace and comfort are intertwined even in the darkest of places. Sometimes we just have to do a better job of paying attention to them. Let God be your light. Allow him to shine in the midst of the ugliness and the clutter. Watch as his light transforms you in ways you never imagined possible. Watch as beauty seeps through the holes of your faith. And watch as he divinely makes everything beautiful in its own time. That's right, everything—the good, the bad, and the ugly.

NOTES

Chapter 1: Wanted: Spiritual Masochists

1. William Hazlitt, *The Round Table: Northcote's Conversations* (London: Bell and Daldy, 1871), 101.

2. John Oswalt, *Isaiah*, NIV Application Commentary (Grand Rapids: Zondervan, 2003).

3. Thomas Merton, *No Man Is an Island* (New York: Harcourt, Brace, 1955), 212–13.

Chapter 2: Confessions of an Imperfect Christian

1. Anne Lamott, *Traveling Mercies* (New York: Pantheon Books, 1999).

2. Martin Luther, "Defense of All the Articles," Lazareth translation, as found in Grace Brame, *Receptive Prayer* (Chalice Press, 1985), 119.

Chapter 3: Conversations with God

1. Joseph Hart, "I Will Go to Jesus," published 1759.

Chapter 5: The Gift of the Broken

1. Frederick Lehman, "The Love of God," published 1919.

2. Ken Gire, *Intimate Moments with the Savior* (Grand Rapids: Zondervan, 1989), 47–49.

Chapter 7: Forgive Us . . . as We Forgive Others

1. CNN, "Amish grandfather: 'We must not think evil of this man,'" CNN.com, October 5, 2006, http://www.cnn.com/2006/US/10/04/amish.shooting/index.html.

2. Ibid.

3. Saint John of the Cross, *The Spiritual Canticle* (Washington, DC: ICS Publishing, 1991).

4. Henri Nouwen, *The Road to Daybreak* (Image, 1990), 61.

Chapter 8: The Demons of Addiction

1. Dr. Gerald May, *Addiction and Grace* (San Francisco: Harper SanFrancisco, 1991), 3–4, 13.

Chapter 9: Is God Enough?

1. Brennan Manning, *The Ragamuffin Gospel* (Portland: Multnomah, 1990), 46.

Chapter 10: The Treasures of Darkness

1. Mother Teresa, *Come Be My Light* (New York: Doubleday, 2007), 192–93.

2. Helen Keller, *Light in My Darkness* (West Chester, PA: Chrysalis Books, 2000), 5.

3. Ibid..

A. J. Gregory is an accomplished freelance writer who has helped author nine books. Thought-provoking and meditative, Gregory is not afraid to seek out and expose the truth of the inner life—the good, bad, and ugly. Through asking the tough questions, her transparency is honest, refreshing, and painfully revealing. *Messy Faith* is her groundbreaking attempt at finding some equilibrium between spirituality and the realities of life. She is a member of The Life Christian Church, a seeker-friendly congregation located in a suburb of New York City.